WORKDAY
PRAYERS

WORKDAY PRAYERS

On-the-Job Meditations for Tending Your Soul

TIMOTHY JONES

LOYOLA PRESS.
CHICAGO

LOYOLAPRESS.

3441 N. ASHLAND AVENUE
CHICAGO, ILLINOIS 60657

Unless otherwise indicated, Scripture quotations are from the New Revised Standard Version Bible: Catholic Edition copyright © 1993 and 1989 by the Division of Christian Education of the National Council of the Churches of Christ in the U.S.A. Used by permission. All rights reserved.

Scripture quotations marked NJB are from the New Jerusalem Bible © 1985 by Darton, Longman & Todd, Ltd., and Doubleday, a division of Bantam Doubleday Dell, Inc. Reprinted by permission.

Scripture quotations marked NIV are from the Holy Bible, New International Version ®. Copyright © 1973, 1978, 1984 by International Bible Society. Used by permission of Zondervan Publishing House. All rights reserved. The "NIV" and "New International Version" trademarks are registered in the United States Trademark Office. Use of either trademark requires the permission of International Bible Society.

Scripture quotations marked KJV are from the King James Version.

Acknowledgements continued on page 265

Cover and interior design by Eileen Wagner

Library of Congress Cataloging-in-Publication Data
Jones, Timothy K., 1955–
      Workday prayers : on-the-job meditations for tending your soul / Timothy.
         p. cm.
      ISBN 0-8294-1375-8 (paperback)
      1. Employees—Prayer-books and devotions—English.
      2.Devotional calendars. I. Title.
    BV4593 .J66 2000
    242'.88—dc21   00-023514
                                  CIP

Printed in Canada
00 01 02 03 04 / 10 9 8 7 6 5 4 3 2 1

CONTENTS

CONTENTS

CONTENTS

CONTENTS

CONTENTS

CONTENTS

CONTENTS

CONTENTS

CONTENTS

CONTENTS

CONTENTS

PRAYER AND WORK

At a stress-filled, deadline-driven time in my life, I discovered an ancient spiritual motto: "Pray and work." Three little words from another time, but they suddenly seemed keenly contemporary. They helped bring sanity to a schedule running out of control. I soon knew I had unearthed a simple prescription for balance amid a harried life. I needed only to carry on in my daily tasks, making sure I did not neglect a deep impulse to turn to God.

When this little motto first began to spread among medieval Europe's monks and spiritual seekers, it was passed along in Latin, with a lilt and rhyme missing in the English: "Ora et labora." St. Benedict, to whom historians trace the genius of the phrase, straddled the fifth and sixth centuries, a time as crowded with stresses and change as ours. Still, Benedict envisioned a life ordered and made rich by both work and prayer. You should get your job done, he said, but not be consumed by it. You should pray, but not to the exclusion of daily responsibilities. As with everything else, work should be given its due, but not more. Ora *et* labora. Pray *and* work.

Whatever the language or era, the motto has rung with clear and practical wisdom. Now, more than ever, we need to recover the riches and rhythms of such a spiritually sane approach. So when I feel impossible schedules breathing down my neck, I remember something: I can do more than slavishly hack away at tasks. I can take a deep breath and invite God in. Sitting at my desk, gathering around a table with others for a meeting, talking to a colleague at a coffeemaker, I can remember that I am not only a worker but also a person of God's making. I can pray, wherever I am, whatever I'm doing. Right in the midst of the day's routines I can inwardly form brief prayers, whispers of praise and longing to the One who is above and within. I work *and* pray.

And when the calm of a sanctuary or woodland glade would make me linger too long, keeping me away from my honest duties, I remember how work has a place too. Especially as it is made holy, made more than a job. For even within the routine of production deadlines and sales reports and meeting agendas I can cultivate the soul. Jesus, after all, worked in a carpenter's shop for most of his life; surely he lived out his relationship with God amid the resinous smells of sawed wood, even the occasional splinter in the finger. To be holy I probably need not sell my living-room furniture and move to a remote cabin retreat. No, I pray *and* work. I live with and for God on common occasions, as someone said. And then, at unexpected moments, the gritty realities of the workplace become a meeting ground, a place of encounter with the divine. Prayer takes root in the particulars of a distasteful task or an encounter with a cranky boss. I find a way to keep at my work, not only giving out, but also pausing, as I labor, to let the soul feed and thrive. I find a way not to let my job eat me alive, as a friend puts it.

If that describes your hope and longing, you are not alone. As a culture we grow hungrier by the year for spiritual realities. And that expectation extends to our careers and workplaces. Spirituality, once a taboo subject for polite company, is making a comeback in our party conversations, TV programs, and yes, factories and offices. We admit out loud that we don't want what philosopher Albert Camus called "soulless work." Why make prayer and work remain separate domains, cordoned off one from another? In a phenomenon often reported in the news media, American corporations now try to boost employee morale by acknowledging the spiritual side of work. Managers at companies—including household names like Bethlehem Steel, Honeywell, and IBM— attend training seminars on merging leadership and spirituality. Whether company policy or not, many of us hunt for resources that benefit our souls, not just our production quotas or annual reviews.

This simple book offers a plan for recovering the presence of the Holy during the nine-to-five (or any shift, any work arrangement). Just as monks have always sanctified

the day's work through the regular set of prayers they call
the Daily Office, you, too, no matter how secular your
surroundings, can adopt a simple prayer discipline.
Combining work and prayer, productivity and spirituality
may be simpler than you ever imagined.

This book provides a good beginning. You will find a
page for each day on the job, containing a short medi-
tation, a prayer, and a simple thought you might come
back to at odd moments. Some of the prayers and meditations come from ancient sages—St. Augustine, St.
Francis of Assisi, Dame Julian of Norwich, George
Herbert, the psalmists. Others come from the pens of
more modern spiritual teachers—Henri Nouwen, Mother
Teresa of Calcutta, Oswald Chambers. All are designed to
help you find your soul at work. No page has more to
read and reflect on than you can easily manage over a
coffee break or as a brief part of your lunch hour. After
all, the simple spiritual discipline offered here is not
meant to compete with your job, only enrich it. Not to
give you an excuse for avoiding a tough project, but to
give you renewed energy and wider perspective. (See also
the conclusion, "Prayer at Work," with its hints for praying on the job.)

At a time when many of us feel pressure to outperform
last year's accomplishments, at a time when downsizing
and layoffs fray nerves of the calmest worker, at a time
when getting along with colleagues seems more difficult

than ever, not neglecting the riches of the spiritual life
makes great sense. If you are eager to find deeper
sources of patience, creativity, and daily staying power,
these prayers and meditations can help. Don't hesitate
to experiment with creating a pattern that suits your situation. Allow for trial and error, even fits and starts. The
important thing is to begin. As prayer and work take their
rightful place, both will become fuller than ever.

WINTER

TO CALM THE SOUL

For most of us, daily life includes the roar of trucks, the clatter of machines, the banter of an office mate, the murmured conversations in a hallway, or the expressway jostle of the daily commute. To speak of a quiet moment for prayer seems like a stretch of the imagination.

But something in us still longs for at least an *inner* place where we can turn to our souls for renewal and reconnection. We long for the ability to pull aside, if only for a moment, to pause and pray. Ask God for help in doing so now.

PRAY

Lord, my heart is not proud
    nor my eyes raised too high.
Neither do I exercise myself in weighty matters
    or in things too profound for me.
Surely I have calmed and quieted my soul
    as a weaned child with its mother;
    my soul is as a weaned child within me.

PSALM 131:1–2, AUTHOR'S TRANSLATION

REMEMBER Learning to pray on the job may not seem easy, but it is possible.

A HEART FOR WHAT MATTERS

Many people today want to go through their workdays with more awareness of what matters. But work has a way of obliterating our best intentions. It seems difficult indeed to stay spiritually mindful when deadlines or quotas or income projections press hard. It is possible, though, at least some of the time, not to forget God.

PRAY

Lord, help me remember you today.
Break into my routine and remind me
that you are worth making room for,
no matter how busy things seem.
Let me find my truest delight in you.
I want to greet gladly your coming into my little world. Amen.

REMEMBER Sometimes all it takes to stay more aware is a simple, gentle decision to open more of our lives and our work times to the Divine Other.

WHEN LIFE HEMS US IN

Sometimes it seems as though life hems us in and shrinks our hearts. Crises weigh us down, and pressures at work wear us out. We feel insignificant, our spirits flat.

At such times we can turn to the One who can invade our little world with expansive, enlarging grace.

PRAY

O Lord, the house of my soul is cramped.

Enlarge it, that you may enter in.

It is in ruins, please restore it!

Parts of it must offend your eyes;

I admit it and know it, but who will cleanse it?

ST. AUGUSTINE, FOURTH/FIFTH CENTURY

REMEMBER "[The Lord] performs wonders for his faithful" (Psalm 4:3, NJB).

DAY BY DAY

Often we do not know what is to come tomorrow or the next day. But we can focus on today, asking God to help us live it fully, freely, faithfully.

PRAY

Thanks be to you,
Lord Jesus Christ,
for all the benefits
that you have won for us,
for all the pains and insults
that you endured for us.

O most merciful Redeemer,
Friend and Brother,
may we know you more clearly,
love you more dearly,
and follow you more nearly,
day by day.

ST. RICHARD OF CHICHESTER, THIRTEENTH CENTURY

REMEMBER "Do not worry about tomorrow, for tomorrow will bring worries of its own. Today's trouble is enough for today" (Matthew 6:34).

WORTHY OF REVERENCE

Sometimes we go through life with an "I've been this way before" dullness. Nothing serves so well as a tonic for a tired soul as a bracing vision of God's greatness. Nothing is quite so humbling.

PRAY

You are God and we praise you;
You are the Lord and we acclaim you. . . .
Father of majesty unbounded,
Your true and only Son worthy of all worship,
And the Holy Spirit advocate and guide.
You are Christ the King of glory,
The eternal Son of the Father.
When you became human to set us free
You did not abhor the virgin's womb.
You overcame the sting of death
And opened the kingdom of heaven to all believers.
You are seated at God's right hand in glory;
We believe that you will come and be our judge.
Come then Lord and help your people,
Bought with the price of your own blood;
And bring us with your saints
To glory everlasting.[1]

TE DEUM, FOURTH CENTURY

REMEMBER Even common moments can shine forth with the glory of God—reminding us to breathe reverent thanks, even in the ordinary round of duty.

THE PEACE WE LONG FOR

The day when the Babe came down,
>   in the midst of the manger stall,
>   the angelic watchers descended and proclaimed, "Peace!"
May that peace be in all my streets
>   for all my children and their children.

ST. EPHRAEM THE SYRIAN, *NISIBENE HYMNS* 4:8, FOURTH CENTURY

PRAY

Lord, help me to remember the simple glories wrapped up in everyday events and ordinary people. May the peace you brought millennia ago in a small child today be mine to experience, mine to share. Amen.

REMEMBER We all long for peace—in our homes and in our streets. Something began long ago when Jesus was born that makes our longing more than a mere possibility. Try to live today in such a way that furthers that reconciling work.

WAITING FOR GOD-WITH-US

Emmanuel is an ancient name—often applied to Jesus—that means "God with us." Does not that name represent the cry of many hearts—that God would come and never leave? Let the name form your prayer today.

PRAY

O come, O come, Emmanuel,
And ransom captive Israel,
That mourns in lonely exile here
Until the Son of God appear.

O come, Thou Wisdom from on high,
Who orderest all things mightily;
To us the path of knowledge show,
And teach us in her ways to go.

O come, Thou Rod of Jesse, free
Thine own from Satan's tyranny;
From depths of hell Thy people save,
And give them victory over the grave.

O come, Desire of nations, bind
In one the hearts of humankind;
Bid Thou our sad divisions cease,
And be Thyself our King of Peace.

NINTH-CENTURY LATIN HYMN; TRANSLATED BY JOHN MASON NEALE, NINETEENTH CENTURY

REMEMBER Wait for God to be with you, to deliver, teach, and bring peace to your day.

MARY'S SONG OF PRAISE

And Mary said,
My soul magnifies the Lord,
And my spirit rejoices in God my Savior.
For he has regarded the humble estate of his handmaiden:
    from henceforth all generations will call me blessed.
For he that is mighty has done to me great things;
    and holy is his name.
And his mercy is on them that fear him from generation
    to generation.
He has shown strength with his arm;
    he has scattered the proud in the imagination of
    their hearts.
He has put down the mighty from their seats,
    and exalted the humble.
He has filled the hungry with good things;
    and the rich he has sent empty away.
He has helped his servant Israel,
    in remembrance of his mercy;
As he spoke to our fathers, to Abraham,
    and to his descendants for ever.

LUKE 1:46–55, KJV, ADAPTED

PRAY

Lord, help me not overlook or neglect those around me who are simple and humble. Remind me how you use those whose heart is inclined toward you, and those who are willing. Amen.

REMEMBER He who is mighty can do great things for you. God rains mercy and strength on those who reverence him, from generation to generation.

WHEN SMALLER IS BETTER

Our culture never ceases to be impressed by the big and showy. "Supersize" and "jumbo" appeal to our quest for value and worth. Marketers know that sheer size can sometimes clinch a sale, in spite of questionable quality. And we assume that where huge crowds flock we will find truly important people or events.

However, "God chose what is foolish in the world to shame the wise; God chose what is weak in the world to shame the strong; God chose what is low and despised in the world, things that are not, to reduce to nothing things that are, so that no one might boast in the presence of God" (1 Corinthians 1:27–29).

PRAY

Lord, I remember that with you the small is often significant. Jesus came to earth as a baby, born in a simple manger, witnessed by only a handful of shepherds and farm animals and traveling sages. When he was an adult, his inner circle numbered only a dozen. Yet how you used him to accomplish great good! Remind me that with your presence within and alongside, great things come from small things. Refresh my memory about how you promise to use me and my little life. Amen.

REMEMBER It is the small, humble, out-of-the-way things—the "little" people and everyday choices—that shape history and carry the day.

THE WONDER OF SIMPLICITY

There is a blessed simplicity to much of the story of Jesus' life. We sometimes overlay it with long words and elaborate theological schemes. All that has a place, in a way. But then we are brought back, every now and then, to the stark simplicity of a child born a king, a ruler nailed to a wooden crossbeam, a Savior who came almost unnoticed among the most sophisticated.

PRAY

Pray, God, keep us simple.

WILLIAM MAKEPEACE THACKERAY, NINETEENTH CENTURY

REMEMBER Is God asking you to become simpler in your approach, more focused on the lasting values that, for all their countercultural lack of guile, matter most?

A BLESSING FOR OUR WORK

Jesus' coming—his incarnation, his birth as a carpenter's son—forever reminds us that work can be graced with holiness and the very presence of God. Is it any accident that the hands that reached out to heal and break bread were strong, callused hands?

PRAY

Bless to me, O God, everything my eye shall see
Bless to me, O God, everything my hand shall do
Bless to me, O God, everything my brain shall think
Bless to me, O God, the place and the equipment.
Bless to me, O God, the people we shall serve through our work.

Be in the interruptions and the setbacks
Be in the eye of the person who is difficult
Be in the eye of the person who is a delight.[2]
TRADITIONAL CELTIC BLESSING

REMEMBER In his day Jesus was commonly called the carpenter, not just the rabbi.

THE EXTRAORDINARY
IN THE ORDINARY

For all the miracles surrounding the birth and life and death of Christ, there is still much that is ordinary. God took a lowly group of peasant people during an era like any other and effected an extraordinary impact. It makes you think about how God might use the ordinary aspects of this day—your job, your contacts, your little aspirations—and bless them with his empowering presence and make them count for more than you would have thought.

PRAY

Child of Glory

Child of Mary

Born in the stable

The King of all

You came to our wasteland

In our place suffered

Draw near to us who to you call.[3]

REMEMBER "God works in moments" (Old French saying).

RUNNING, ALWAYS RUNNING

Sometimes we go through life and work on a kind of automatic pilot. We race from this task to that, rushing from minor accomplishment to minor accomplishment, hoping always that we are running toward success. So we groggily greet our family as we hustle out the door. We don't notice the morning sky on our trip into work. Or we bump into someone at work, ask how things are going, and then fail to look into that person's eyes to read the subtler signals that convey the answer.

PRAY

Lord, when my memories of your promised power grow cold, when my hope for change goes dormant, when my eyes glaze over with indifference, come with your Spirit. Rekindle my faith; renew my zeal. Forgive what is lacking in me, and draw forth what can be. Let me live with greater awareness of all that you want to be to me and do through me. Give me new energy to live and to shine to your glory, through Jesus Christ the Lord. Amen.

REMEMBER How can you slow down today and appreciate your life, appreciate those around you?

LOOKING AHEAD

Companies and workplaces of any sort often are forced to look ahead. Consultants may come in with elaborate techniques for forecasting trends and anticipating changes. The future holds a peculiar fascination because we know that today will inevitably feed into tomorrow in ways we may not foresee and certainly cannot control.

Where do you see your life headed—five years from now, for example? And what about your ultimate destination?

PRAY

Lord, take me where you want me to go. Let my choices reflect your purposes for me. And when all is said and done, I want you to be waiting for me at journey's end. I pray this very old prayer for myself:

God be with you today and forever
Jesus be in you to pardon and tether
Spirit be on you and leave you never....

That you may be as free as the wind,
As soft as a sheep's wool,
As straight as an arrow,
And that you may journey into the heart of God.[4]

REMEMBER Are you journeying into the future that God wants to create through you and for you?

CLEARING THE CLUTTER

Every life in our modern society contains a certain amount of clutter. Whether your work space is tidy or mounded with stuff, one kind of clutter seems to affect most everyone: the distractions of a life crowded with too many sounds, activities, and involvements.

PRAY

Turn me around, O God.
Turn me away from the distractions of a cluttered life.
Turn me toward your clear invitation to approach you.
Help me to be single in focus
    willing in spirit
        and reachable in my inmost self
that you might find praise on my lips and obedience in
my intentions.
Amen.

REMEMBER Amid the discord and disquiet, how might a moment of silence help you today?

AS WE WALK GOD'S WAY

When we answer God's invitation to follow his way, God gives us no guarantees that we will have an uneventful trip. We may have to negotiate twists and turns we do not expect, even detours and roadblocks. We may grow weary. But still we can pray; always we can turn to the One who walks before, beside, and ahead of us.

PRAY

Lord, you are taking me into territory I have never seen or imagined. Sometimes the path seems tougher than I expected. Sometimes I feel tempted to veer off and follow a side trail. But then you remind me that I can keep going, that the way will always, somehow, open up ahead of me.

REMEMBER "Lead me, O LORD, in your righteousness because of my enemies; make your way straight before me" (Psalm 5:8).

THE PLACE OF TRUST

Trust in the LORD and do good;
>   dwell in the land and enjoy safe pasture.
Delight yourself in the LORD
>   and he will give you the desires of your heart.
Commit your way to the LORD;
>   trust in him and he will do this:
He will make your righteousness shine like the dawn,
>   the justice of your cause like the noonday sun.

PSALM 37:3–6, NIV

PRAY

When I come to you, Lord, I often bring many feelings and atti-
tudes. Today I want to come in trust. Give me courage founded in
you. Help me find my confidence in your good purposes. Help me
in my fears not flinch from committing my life to your unfailing
goodness and trustworthy plans.

REMEMBER "The LORD is good to those whose hope is in him"
(Lamentations 3:25, NIV).

IN SEARCH OF
OUR RIGHTFUL MIND

Sometimes the push and pull of deadlines or production quotas or demanding clients leaves us frantic and frazzled. We get so sucked into work that it becomes a taskmaster, relentlessly obliterating our sense of quiet, our awareness of God. If we can get still for just a moment, however, we can ask for God's help—and calming, renewing sweetness.

PRAY

Dear Lord and Father of mankind,
Forgive our foolish ways;
Reclothe us in our rightful mind,
In purer lives Thy service find,
In deeper reverence, praise.

In simple trust like theirs who heard,
Beside the Syrian sea,
The gracious calling of the Lord,
Let us, like them, without a word,
Rise up and follow Thee.

Drop Thy still dews of quietness,
Till all our strivings cease;
Take from our souls the strain and stress,
And let our ordered lives confess
The beauty of Thy peace.

JOHN GREENLEAF WHITTIER, NINETEENTH CENTURY

REMEMBER If we can get still for just a moment, we can ask for God's help.

THE MUSIC OF THE UNIVERSE

In most jobs, the details of work sometimes become monotonous. Even the rattle of office work or the predictable coffee-break conversations take on a droning sameness. But there are other sounds to listen to as we move through the day. We cock our soul's ears for a kind of heavenly chorus, beyond the wavelength of normal hearing—an echo of the worship that goes on continually in the celestial realms.

PRAY

May none of God's wonderful works
keep silence, night or morning.
Bright stars, high mountains, the depths of the seas,
sources of rushing rivers:
May all these break into song as we sing
to Father, Son, and Holy Spirit.
May all the angels in the heavens reply:
Amen! Amen! Amen!
Power, praise, honor, eternal glory
to God, the only giver of grace.
Amen! Amen! Amen!

AUTHOR UNKNOWN

REMEMBER "The human soul is a silent harp in God's choir, whose strings need only to be swept by the divine breath to chime in with the harmonies of creation" (Henry David Thoreau, nineteenth century).

WHEN YOU HAVE TO WAIT

In our day of instant everything, few things drive us to distraction as much as having to wait. We impatiently wait in checkout lines at the supermarket or look frequently in the mailbox for that important letter.

Our relationship with God entails waiting, too. Some of the most profound changes in how we pray or relate to difficult people come through fits and starts. Even if a conversion or insight overtakes us suddenly, giving the change flesh and bone takes energy, patience, and willingness to keep at it.

PRAY

O loving Father, I confess that I do not often wait patiently or well. I am anxious to see some things happen today, tomorrow, this week. Help me to be anxious most of all to see and know you. Help me to trust you always and in everything.

REMEMBER "It is good that one should wait quietly for the salvation of the LORD" (Lamentations 3:26).

ONLY THROUGH ENDURANCE

We are apt to think of conversion as a onetime, cataclysmic event. Sometimes it truly is; the "before" and "after" snapshots reveal nothing less than startling change. But our conversion unfolds in years as often as it does in highly charged instants. There needs to be a steadiness to it, a slow burn, not just an explosive start.

Growth in holiness will have us stepping from stone to stone, from quiet revelation to quiet revelation. That need not make us question the reality of our unfolding grasp of God and God's ways with us. It means only that we resolve to keep at it today, tomorrow, for all of life, as God makes us able. Conversion becomes a continuing process, one we live out in the lunchrooms, hallways, and parking lots of our jobs, day in and day out.

PRAY

Lord, I move forward only to fall back. I see something clearly only to find myself blind to the truth in another setting. I want to continue to grow steadily into the person you want me to be. Show me how. Give me strength. Keep me at it. Amen.

REMEMBER "Nothing great was ever accomplished without much enduring" (St. Catherine of Siena, fourteenth century).

THE PROMISE OF A NEW DAY

We often begin a new day, new week, or new season with the feeling that everything depends on us. We fear that without our ingenuity things will fall flat. It is no wonder that an obligation to make things "happen" drives us. So we bank on what we can achieve and overlook what we can only receive. While energizing for a time, such an approach ultimately wearies us. It burdens and burns us out. But there is another way.

PRAY

O Lord our God, under the shadow of your wings
let us find hope.
You support us both when we are young
and when our hair goes gray.
When our strength is in you it is strength indeed,
but when our own, it is weakness.
And we return to you
that from our weariness our souls may rise to you....
For within you is refreshment and our true strength.
ST. AUGUSTINE, FOURTH/FIFTH CENTURY

REMEMBER We can undertake any new venture—or any new day—aware of unseen forces at work, alert to a gracious God who works to bring good out of every moment.

THE PROMISE
THAT KEEPS US WARM

Sometimes winter, with its cold days and long nights, leaves us discouraged, hardly able to believe that spring will again warm our hearts. The title of one book says it well: *The Winter of Our Discontent*. We may forget the glorious changes spring promises. But the promise of warmth and sunshine allows us to endure winter's nights.

PRAY

Lord, I do not always remember that you are a God of light and warming goodness. Remind me that winter turns always to spring, nighttime ever rotates to morning, and my most desolate moments can bring me ultimately to awareness of your constancy and goodness.

REMEMBER "[My people] shall come and sing aloud on the height of Zion, and they shall be radiant over the goodness of the LORD. . . . Their life shall become like a watered garden, and they shall never languish again. . . . I will turn their mourning into joy, I will comfort them, and give them gladness for sorrow" (Jeremiah 31:12–13).

THE AWFUL WAIT

Next to times of suffering, moments of waiting may reveal to us the most about the genuineness of our faith. Waiting tries our patience to the nth degree and tests our confidence in God to the uttermost. Sometimes waiting is agonizing, nothing less than a heartbreaking trial of fortitude: a woman praying for her son, incarcerated for twenty years; a young man trying to break the demon of chemical dependency; a rejected lover yearning for a hint of affection; a middle-aged worker stuck in a suffocating job.

PRAY

O Lord, all my longing is known to you;
my sighing is not hidden from you. . . .
But it is for you, O LORD, that I wait;
it is you, O LORD my God, who will answer.
For I pray, "Only do not let them rejoice over me,
those who boast against me when my foot slips."
For I am ready to fall,
and my pain is ever with me.

PSALM 38:9, 15–17

REMEMBER "Every delay is hateful, but it gives much wisdom" (Publilius Syrus, first century).

WHY PRAYERS MATTER

Sometimes when we pray, we fight the nagging fear that such time is wasted—or is at least an interruption of what really matters. But because in prayer we invite an infinitely powerful and intimately loving God into everyday situations, our simple, faltering prayers may accomplish more than we can imagine.

PRAY

Gracious God, I thank you that when I call out,
* you bend down your ear to listen.*
You promise to respond,
* even when I don't see all the ways and effects and outcomes.*
Remind me that time spent in your presence always matters,
* always brings good. Amen.*

REMEMBER "Whoever flees prayer flees all that is good" (St. John of the Cross, sixteenth century).[5]

THE CHAPEL OF THE HEART

It is not necessary for being with God to be always at church; we may make a chapel of our heart, wherein to retire from time to time, to converse with Him in meekness, humility, and love. Every one is capable of such familiar conversation with God, some more, some less: He knows what we can do. Let us begin then; perhaps He expects but one generous resolution on our part.

BROTHER LAWRENCE, SIXTEENTH CENTURY, ADAPTED

PRAY

Lord, I want not to hold back
*   or be stingy in my time spent relating to you.*
Help me to turn to you frequently today.
Let me be unstinting in my openness to you
*   and your presence.*

REMEMBER Prayer can be offered in any circumstance in any kind of moment. Take breathers today that allow you to send up simple, spontaneous, heartfelt prayers.

GETTING DOWN THE RHYTHM

Sometimes we are tempted to concentrate on one side or the other: elbow grease or quiet devotions. But we need not settle for an either/or—not when we remember that our work, by itself, will never effect the world's transformation. Not when we realize that our prayer, apart from good deeds, is empty sentiment. No, the trick is in the right rhythm, the appropriate balance. We pray but also work. We pull away from the press of life but then throw ourselves into fighting the chaos. We give our efforts our best and then leave them in God's capable hands.

PRAY

Here am I, Lord. Send me.

REMEMBER "Work as if you were to live a hundred years, and pray as if you were to die tomorrow" (Benjamin Franklin, eighteenth century).

THE PROMISE OF
THE SLOW AND STEADY

We are "quickaholics," someone once said, infatuated with the fast and efficient. Now always seems preferable to later, the quick fix more desirable than waiting for lasting resolution. But some things—such as cultivating a deeper life or stronger relationships—take time. Not losing hope requires a long view beyond the present tense.

PRAY

Lord, so many areas in my life seem urgent.
Half the time I feel antsy and anxious.
I have grown unaccustomed to waiting.
Sometimes I stop believing that what I cannot see
will someday come to be.
But I want to be patient.
Let me trust you and your timing.
Through him who learned to trust you for everything,
Jesus Christ. Amen.

REMEMBER Knowing the end result helps us stay steady in the moment at hand. Recall that the apostle Paul told a young church centuries ago, "I am quite confident that the One who began a good work in you will go on completing it until the Day of Jesus Christ comes" (Philippians 1:6, NJB).

THE SOURCE AND GOAL OF OUR WORK

The fruit of silence is prayer.
The fruit of prayer is faith.
The fruit of faith is love.
The fruit of love is service.
The fruit of service is peace.[6]
MOTHER TERESA OF CALCUTTA, TWENTIETH CENTURY

PRAY

Lord, help me want to make room for you. As I do, allow me to hear, to know, to care, to follow. May your peace sustain me and empower me to do far more than I could ever hope to accomplish on my own. Amen.

REMEMBER Let today have at least a moment of silence, knowing that from it can grow much fruit, steadying goodness, and secure peace.

LIGHT IN OUR EYES

Light is above us, and color around us; but if we have not light and color in our eyes, we will not perceive them outside us.
JOHANN WOLFGANG VON GOETHE, EIGHTEENTH/NINETEENTH CENTURY

PRAY

O most loving Father,

who wants us to give thanks for all things,

to dread nothing but the loss of you,

and to place on you all our concerns,

keep us from faithless fears and worldly anxieties,

and grant that no clouds of our daily life

will hide from us the light of that love that is immortal,

and that you have shown us in your Son, Jesus Christ our Lord.

Amen.

WILLIAM BRIGHT, TWENTIETH CENTURY, ADAPTED

REMEMBER Much of what we see has less to do with the circumstances and situations around us and more to do with cultivating our eyesight.

EVERYWHERE, ALL THE TIME

Theologians use a fancy term to describe a feature of God that inspires our wonder: *omnipresence*. That means that God can be and is everywhere—all the time. When today's challenges seem to refute that old idea, remind yourself that Someone always sees, always goes with, always stands near to help.

PRAY

Christ as a light
illumine and guide me!
Christ as a shield
overshadow and protect me!
Christ be under me! Christ be over me!
Christ be beside me, on left hand and right!
Christ be before me, behind me, around me!
Christ, this day, be within and without me!
ST. PATRICK, FIFTH CENTURY

REMEMBER "God is within all things, but not included; outside all things, but not excluded; above all things, but not beyond their reach" (St. Gregory the Great, sixth century).

NO NEED TO DRAW BACK

Most of us have spiritual longings, but we wonder if we dare follow them. Will God receive us gladly? Can we pray as we are?

Love bade me welcome, yet my soul drew back
    Guilty of dust and sin.
But quick-eyed love, observing me grow slack,
    From my first entrance in,
Drew nearer to me, sweetly questioning,
    If I lacked anything.
GEORGE HERBERT, SEVENTEENTH CENTURY

PRAY

Lord, I need a fresh reminder that you are a God of mercy and grace. Yes, you expect righteousness and goodness from me, but why do I sometimes think that you demand perfection? Keep telling me that whatever your judging, awesome holiness, you are also a God of love. Amen.

REMEMBER Prayer may lead us far along to a new place, but always we begin where we are, as we are.

THE SOUL'S FOOD

Everyone's stomach and bloodstream need sustenance and replenishment. It is no wonder that the Bible sometimes speaks of our being hungry for righteousness. Or that some of the great saints and mystics of the church speak of humanity's gnawing spiritual hunger.

Think of the kind of food your soul needs in order to get by today. Ask God for a spiritual daily bread—all that you need to carry on the life of faith and service God calls forth from you.

PRAY

Lord, you are my sustenance,
the bread of life.
May I feed fully, without hurry.
Amen.

REMEMBER Spiritual junk food—high in euphoric calories but lacking in substance—may assuage our appetite for a time. But we need life-giving bread that feeds the soul's deepest hunger.

A LIGHT IN THE DARK

One thing is certain: Every life contains dark moments. We live in a world in which we cannot long escape reminders of others' dark deeds. It is no wonder that the Bible speaks so often of light. Jesus even defined his life and ministry in terms of light breaking in: "I am the light of the world," he said (John 8:12).

Pause now to consider what dark areas in you or dark situations around you need Christ's bright light to shine. How will that light make a difference? What will it reveal? What shadowy actions will it drive away?

PRAY

Lord, you dwell in light.
You not only dwell in light, you are light,
*   and the light of my world.*
Please shine, and let me see. Amen.

REMEMBER "Light, even though it passes through pollution, is not polluted" (St. Augustine, fourth/fifth century).

NOT TO FLINCH BUT TO FOLLOW

Sometimes, when presented with a tough choice requiring action, we are genuinely puzzled. The answer seems long in coming, and even then we feel we cannot settle all uncertainty. But more often than not, we *know* what goodness requires and where God's guidance points. What we need is not so much clarity as courage.

PRAY

Lord, I want to be found faithful. Assist me in doing your will. Let me not flinch in doing what your way and what everyday compassion require. Keep me from cheap substitutes for heartfelt following. Amen.

REMEMBER "What does it profit you to give God one thing if he asks of you another? Consider what it is God wants, and then do it. You will as a result satisfy your heart better than with something toward which you yourself are inclined" (St. John of the Cross, sixteenth century).[7]

BACK TO BASICS

When we pray, far more important than the words we use (or stumble over) is a simple decision to come. *That* we pray matters more than what we say. Prayer begins when we pay attention to the soul's restlessness that draws us to prayer, and then when we do something, no matter how elemental, to respond. We sit down perhaps. Or we pause and look out the office window. Or we close our eyes on the noisy subway. And then, however haltingly, we speak. We address God, unworried about perfection, concerned only that our heart is pointed in the right direction.

PRAY

Gracious God, who invites me always and everywhere to come to you by asking, seeking, and knocking, keep me from getting caught up in the minor points and little issues. Help me come to you with my whole heart and without anxiety. In the name of Jesus, who lived a life of prayer. Amen.

REMEMBER "Ask, and it will be given you; search, and you will find; knock, and the door will be opened for you. For everyone who asks receives, and everyone who searches finds, and for everyone who knocks, the door will be opened" (Jesus, in Matthew 7:7–8).

A WORD LIKE NO OTHER

If God's Word is so full of consolations, what overflowing springs shall we find in God himself? If the promise is so sweet, what will the performance be?
RICHARD BAXTER, SEVENTEENTH CENTURY

PRAY

Lord, thank you for not leaving me adrift, without guidance. Thank you for your revealed truth through your inspired witnesses throughout biblical history. May Scripture's written words become living words. Remind me to expect not only insight but also encounter with you. As I hear or think about new truths this week, help me attend to your ways and watch for the fulfillment of your promises. Amen.

REMEMBER "We are to pray during our reading [of the Bible] so that God might help us to properly understand himself and his will and open to us one door after another into his Word" (Philipp Jacob Spener, seventeenth century).

CULTIVATING QUIET IN A NOISY PLACE

Sometimes our words get in the way of what we want to express or do. We may pile them on even after they cease being truly wise or thought out. In these times, silence is usually more helpful to others than our words. "In quietness and in confidence shall be your strength," the Old Testament prophet said (Isaiah 30:15, KJV). On the job today, in what may be a wordy, noisy world, consider ways to nurture a silence that gives others room to speak, that gives God room to move.

PRAY

O Lord, the Scripture says, "there is a time for silence and a time for speech." Savior, teach me the silence of humility, the silence of wisdom, the silence of love, the silence of perfection, the silence that speaks without words, the silence of faith.

Lord, teach me to silence my own heart that I may listen to the gentle movement of the Holy Spirit within me and sense the depths which are of God.

FRANKFURT PRAYER, SIXTEENTH CENTURY

REMEMBER "Eloquent silence is often better than eloquent speech" (Jewish proverb).

THE DRAWBACK OF URGENCY

Urgency seems to be a hallmark of our time. We do fewer and fewer things at a leisurely pace: Fast food has replaced quiet dining; we say, "I need it now" more often than "Take your time"; convenience (often a synonym for *quickness*) has overtaken quality as a virtue. Such pressure seems to affect everything we do, sometimes even how we pray.

PRAY

Today, dear God,
Guide my hopes and selfish schemes
to peer beyond the in-betweens.
Then steer my love to life around me.
Each day, all day, help me to stay
In pace with you.
Can you help, heal?
Slow me down, make me real?
Dear God, today I pray you will.

CHRIS MAXWELL

REMEMBER If the powerful God of the universe is constantly at work in the world—and our lives—we can afford not to rush, not to worry too much.

WHEN PRAYER SEEMS LACKING

When our sense of God's closeness dries up, whether from busyness or from reasons we cannot name, we may fear that prayer is not happening when we try to pray. We suspect that, minus heartfelt warmth, our efforts count for nothing. But prayer hinges on far more than how we feel. Whether the soul feels exuberant or dormant, the *act* of praying is what matters most.

PRAY

God of certainty and steady truth, remind me that you are glad for me to come, whether I am full of fire or I am feeling cold. Let my prayer this day be to you a freely given act of praise and devotion. Amen.

REMEMBER "The most desirable prayer is that where we can quite pour out our soul and freely talk with God. But it is not this alone which is acceptable to him. 'Love [the] one,' said a holy man, 'that perseveres in dry duty.' Beware of thinking that even this is labor lost. God does much work in the heart even at those seasons" (John Wesley, eighteenth century).

A SIMPLER HEART

You can say yes to too much and lose sight of the point and purpose. Add too many good things to your schedule and they cease to be good, for they smother the soul and leave your spirit unwell.

PRAY

Lord, sometimes my life seems like a suitcase
*   crammed so full it is hard to close.*
Sometimes my simplest plans gets thwarted
*   by an onslaught of things to do,*
*   obligations to meet,*
*   expectations to rise to.*
Have I perhaps promised others (and myself) too much?
Do I pack too much into my waking days?
I want not just to do and achieve,
*   but to be still and receive.*
I know that will take a simple heart.

REMEMBER We are born into simplicity, someone once said, but we die of complications.

ANTIDOTE FOR HURRY AND FLURRY

Sometimes, when the work piles up and the deadlines scream, we dash around. We think that we can reduce the mountain of tasks by speeding up and pushing harder. But rushing seldom makes us more productive (research studies show this). And the hurry and flurry hurt our soul. Prayer may help us here. Thinking about God doesn't wave a magic wand over the load of work, but it reminds us that we need not face the work alone.

PRAY

Answer me when I call, O God of my right!
You gave me room when I was in distress.
Be gracious to me, and hear my prayer.
PSALM 4:1

REMEMBER When you feel a bout of "hurry anxiety" coming on, let God gently remind you that God has things well in hand.

WORRIED?

Are you afraid of something today? Worries seem inevitably to haunt us. Not all the time, but often enough that we get distracted. Fear and anxiety typically masquerade under the name of "responsibility" or "foresight" or "realism." But in reality they make us tighten up. They make it harder to reach out to God. They make us hold on to ourselves in stinginess when we are around others.

There is another way: Bathing—or at least punctuating—our day with prayer reminds us that we are not alone. One who knows us and our needs goes with us and works in our circumstances.

PRAY

I want to trust you, Lord. Let confidence in you crowd out my anxious thoughts for the future. Help me to live more deeply aware that a gracious, powerful God is working out his purposes in ways that mean I need not worry.

REMEMBER "Therefore do not worry, saying, 'What will we eat?' or 'What will we drink?' or 'What will we wear?' For it is the Gentiles who strive for all these things; and indeed your heavenly Father knows that you need all these things. . . . So do not worry about tomorrow, for tomorrow will bring worries of its own. Today's trouble is enough for today" (Jesus, in Matthew 6:31–32, 34).

STAYING POWER
AMID THE ROUTINE

Drudgery is one of the finest touchstones of character there is. Drudgery is work that is very far removed from anything to do with the ideal—the utterly mean grubby things; and when we come in contact with them we know instantly whether or not we are spiritually real.[8]

OSWALD CHAMBERS, TWENTIETH CENTURY

PRAY

Lord, help me when the job gets dull, when it takes energy and willpower just to stay put at my desk, table, bench. Save me from dreary monotony. Help me to find riches in the everyday routine, even the distasteful task. Let my work be pleasing to you and helpful to others. I want to remember that I do this not just for me, my boss, or my family, but I do it for you and for my neighbor. Amen.

REMEMBER Even little things, when done with a willing heart, have great and hidden power.

NO EXIT?

When you're trying urgently to get off a freeway or interstate highway, seeing a No Exit sign heightens your anxiety. In other areas, too, our worst fears grow out of thinking there might be no way out: habits that seem unshakable, temptations that seem irresistible, destructive relationships that seem inescapable. Nothing leads us to cave in to despair as much as seeing no hope of a way through.

PRAY

Lord, I need help with seemingly unconquerable impulses or attitudes or habits. This day, please, remind me of your gracious strength. Let me see for myself how you assist me when I try to be faithful. Open doors for me, and put me on a right way. Let me never fear that there's not a way off a wrong road. In the name of Jesus, who blazed the way forward. Amen.

REMEMBER "No testing has overtaken you that is not common to everyone. God is faithful, and he will not let you be tested beyond your strength, but with the testing he will also provide the way out so that you may be able to endure it" (1 Corinthians 10:13).

A SIMPLE OFFERING

Offer yourself by degrees and as you are able . . . to worship God, to beg his grace, to offer him your heart from time to time, in the midst of your business, even every moment if you can. Do not always scrupulously confine yourself to certain rules, or particular forms of devotion; but act with a general confidence in God, with love and humility.

BROTHER LAWRENCE, SIXTEENTH CENTURY

PRAY

Lord, I want to offer you this day my work,
> *my thoughts,*
>> *my intentions,*
>>> *my self.*

May I not hold back from giving you your due.
Guide me to places and people
> *where I can serve you in ways both little and large.*

REMEMBER "I appeal to you therefore, brothers and sisters, by the mercies of God, to present your bodies as a living sacrifice, holy and acceptable to God, which is your spiritual worship" (Romans 12:1).

OUR INEVITABLE TESTIMONY

"Don't parade your piety before others" is an often-quoted dictum about faith. Because of it, we may forget the legitimate place our deeds and generosity have in testifying to God's grace. No one is to brag, of course, and we never do good for show. But Jesus reminded us that a lamp is not hidden under a basket. Be aware that, as you go about your duties today, people will be watching. Someone may be making conclusions about the faith because of what he or she sees in another person—in you. Who you are and what you do inevitably communicate what you believe.

PRAY

Lord, I don't want my witness to you to be full of pomp and circumstance. Yet neither do I want to have so little to show for my faith that others detect no evidence of your presence in me. Help me to live for you, and may my faith overflow into my life, that others may see your goodness.

REMEMBER "Through the testing of this ministry you glorify God by your obedience to the confession of the gospel of Christ and by the generosity of your sharing with them and with all others" (2 Corinthians 9:13).

DOWNWARD MOBILITY

"Stick by your guns." "Stand up for your rights." "Don't let folks walk all over you." These are the slogans and watchwords of our day. In many circumstances we need to do as they say. But as often as not, we need not stand up for our rights but kneel in prayer and go out in humble service. We practice what someone has called *downward* mobility.

PRAY

Lord, help me to love you with all my heart and soul and mind and strength and to love my neighbor as myself. As I try to do that, I want to hear your guidance as to how I should live and ways I should give. Let me be unafraid to descend from what many would see as prestige and having "arrived" and in so doing discover true freedom and deeper fulfillment.

REMEMBER "Do not be ashamed to serve others for the love of Jesus Christ and to seem poor in this world. Do not be self-sufficient but place your trust in God. Do what lies in your power and God will aid your good will" (Thomas à Kempis, fourteenth/fifteenth century).

WHERE WE GET EXPERIENCE

"Wise decisions on the job," someone once said, "come only from experience." But where, he went on to muse, do we gain experience? "Bad decisions."

PRAY

Let me be bold and courageous today, Lord. I am prone to be careful, to mince my words and guard my actions. In many ways, of course, such circumspection saves me embarrassment or even disaster. But I confess that it also holds me back. Let me not be so measured that I hang back from the opportunities you give. Make me unafraid to fail when you seem to be nudging me on. Give me a holy winsomeness and a willingness to let good things "run wild" under your watchful eye. Amen.

REMEMBER "A good life makes a person wise according to God and gives him or her experience in many things, for the more humble he or she is and the more subject to God, the wiser and the more at peace he or she will be in all things" (Thomas à Kempis, fourteenth/fifteenth century).

WHAT NOT TO CARE ABOUT

Happy are those
  who do not follow the advice of the wicked.
Or take the path that sinners tread,
  or sit in the seat of scoffers;
but their delight is in the law of the LORD,
  and on his law they meditate day and night.
They are like trees
  planted by streams of water,
which yield their fruit in its season,
  and their leaves do not wither.

PSALM 1:1–3

PRAY

Lord, when it comes to the choices I will make today, help me to care supremely about what you think. There may be some who try to influence me to do wrong, some who even ridicule the concerns of my conscience. But here you are, telling me that it is in you and through following you that I will be most secure.

REMEMBER We may worry about what other people think, but in an ultimate sense we play our lives out before an Audience of One.

THERE'S ALWAYS TIME

We may think that we cannot possibly finish all the things that crowd our to-do lists. Perhaps we can't. At such times it helps to recall the life of Jesus. For all his busy ministry of healing, for all the urgency of his calling, he never seemed to rush. When he heard that his friend Lazarus had died, one early eyewitness tells us, even then he did not hurry: "Jesus loved . . . Lazarus. Yet when he heard that Lazarus was sick, he stayed where he was two more days" (John 11:5–6, NIV). Jesus carried on with the tasks God put in front of him, knowing that it would be that much longer before he could arrive and call Lazarus back to life. Still he remained steady and faithful.

PRAY

Lord, my list of things to do gets more and more intimidating. I cannot imagine completing all that is expected by my bosses, my family, my friends, and even me. Please help me concentrate on the task before me and not let all the undone jobs rob me of the ability to accomplish what you have for me to do—here and now.

REMEMBER God has made the day, this day, every day. What he has made he calls good. You will have the time you need for what matters most.

JUST HOW URGENT *IS* IT?

When we are in the middle of the stress of deadlines and demands, everything seems urgent. It seems as though nothing can wait. We feel pressed down, stressed out, tied up. Sometimes it helps to ask, "Is all this really that urgent? Is it worth damaging my health? shortchanging my loved ones?" Questions such as those may lead us to say, "It's not!" Then we ask for God's grace to help us become saner, more balanced persons.

PRAY

Lord, I want not to be driven by tasks this day
  as much as drawn by you through them.
Let me work hard,
  but not frantically;
responsibly,
  but not anxiously.
Let me be motivated,
  but not obsessed.
Let me do my work as unto you. Amen.

REMEMBER Sometimes what seems all-powerfully important (and anxiety producing) assumes a different cast when we stop to pray and remember that God promises to be with us through all our work.

WHAT—AND WHOM— DO WE PRAISE?

Whosoever praises God for his essential goodness, and not merely because of the benefits he has bestowed, does really love God for God's sake, and not selfishly. . . . The third degree of love . . . is to love God on his own account, solely because he is God.

ST. BERNARD OF CLAIRVAUX, TWELFTH CENTURY

PRAY

Lord, help me to love you and serve you this day without concern for my rights. Let me not become consumed with getting what I think I deserve. Allow me not to get caught up in worrying whether my contributions get noticed by colleagues. Even more, I want not to turn to you thinking only of what you will give. Give me grace to concern myself with loftier things today.

REMEMBER When we consider God in all his matchless splendor, we are less likely to get caught up in our sometimes petty wishes and whims. Our response becomes one of adoring awe—and loving submission.

A SONG OF HEALTH AND SALVATION

What better way to begin—or renew—the day than to remember the God who has given us breath, who makes the body do its miraculous work, who gives us the ability to dream and carry out plans.

PRAY

Praise to the Lord, the Almighty, the King of creation!
O my soul, praise Him, for He is thy health and salvation!
All ye who hear, now to His temple draw near;
Praise Him in glad adoration.

Praise to the Lord, Who over all things so wondrously reigneth,
Shelters thee under His wings, yea, so gently sustaineth!
Hast thou not seen how thy desires ever have been
Granted in what He ordaineth?

Praise to the Lord, who doth prosper thy work and defend thee;
Surely His goodness and mercy here daily attend thee.
Ponder anew what the Almighty can do,
If with His love He befriend thee.

Praise to the Lord, O let all that is in me adore Him!
All that hath life and breath, come now with praises before Him.
Let the Amen sound from His people again,
Gladly for all we adore Him.

JOACHIM NEANDER, 1680; TRANSLATED BY CATHERINE WINKWORTH IN 1863

REMEMBER The God we admire and adore wants to befriend us.

OUR CONSTANT HELP

Sometimes the sheer vastness of the universe makes us worry that God might not notice us. Amid such limitless stretches of time and space, can God really care about our comparatively little lives?

PRAY

O God, our help in ages past,
Our hope for years to come,
Our shelter from the stormy blast,
And our eternal home.

Before the hills in order stood,
Or earth received her frame,
From everlasting to everlasting thou are God,
To endless years the same.

A thousand ages in thy sight
Are like an evening gone;
Short as the watch that ends the night,
Before the rising sun.

O God our help in ages past,
Our hope for years to come,
Be thou our guide while life shall last,
And our eternal home!

ISAAC WATTS, SEVENTEENTH/EIGHTEENTH CENTURY

REMEMBER We need not worry; the God of eternity is also the God of this moment. The God of the universe is Lord of us.

THE GOAL OF THE JOURNEY

Amid life's common hassles and stresses is always One who accompanies, One to whom we can always turn. And when we do, we find God not only there but also already at work, already in us, already bringing some good out of our situation.

PRAY

You who are full of compassion, in whom I exist, love, and understand; I commit and commend myself to you. Be the goal of my journey and my resting place by the road. From the crowding turmoil of worldly thoughts let my soul find shelter beneath the shadow of your wings. Let my heart, this sea of restless waves, find peace in you, O God.... For you are the wellspring of life and the light of eternal brightness, through whom the just ones who love you live. Let it be to me according to your word.
ST. AUGUSTINE, FOURTH/FIFTH CENTURY, ADAPTED

REMEMBER Our sometimes turbulent hearts find calm in God, our souls a safe place in the shadow of God's wings.

THE RIGHT ANXIETY

Usually anxiety robs us of joy and distracts us from more important things to think about. But there is one anxiety that carries great benefits to the heart and soul: eager, fervent concern to love and know God.

PRAY

We love you, our God, and we want to love you more and more.... O dearest Friend, who has so loved and saved us, the thought of whom is sweet and always growing sweeter, come with Christ and dwell in our hearts; then you will keep a watch over our lips, our steps, our deeds, and we will not need to be anxious either for our souls or our bodies.... O most loving Father of Jesus Christ, from whom flows all love, let our hearts, frozen in sin, cold to you and cold to others, be warmed by this divine fire. Help and bless us. Amen.

ST. ANSELM, ELEVENTH CENTURY, ADAPTED

REMEMBER "Grant to us that we may love you as much as we long to, and as much as we ought" (St. Anselm, eleventh century, adapted).

OPEN TO THE WORLD

Prayer has its drawbacks. Sometimes it drives us further into ourselves, encouraging introspection or self-absorption. It can serve to reinforce our prejudices and make us smaller, not bigger, people; more withdrawn, not more generous. But praying specifically for others can lift our gaze from ourselves and widen the horizons of our view.

Spend some time today considering the needs of others. Pause now and through the day to turn your thoughts into prayers.

PRAY

We bring before you, O Lord,
the troubles and dangers of people and countries,
the sighing of prisoners and oppressed,
the sorrows of the grieving,
the needs of strangers,
the helplessness of the weak,
the depression of the weary,
the failing abilities of the aged.
O Lord, draw near to each; for the sake of Jesus Christ our Lord.

ST. ANSELM, ELEVENTH CENTURY, ADAPTED

REMEMBER Concern for matters of the Spirit should not insulate or isolate us but make us more caring, more generous, more open to a world of need. It is rare to come to God without coming away with heightened sensitivity to others.

OUTMANEUVERING THE CUNNING

We hope in many things—a diploma, a job, a friendship, a move to a new company. But when others seem out to do us harm, we need inner resources, not just outer rearrangements. It is only natural in such times to reach for God's hand and powerful help.

PRAY

Teach us, Holy Father,

> *to hope in your name, from whom all that exists comes.*

Although you are the highest in high heaven,

> *and the holy one among all of heaven's ranks of the holy,*
>> *open our eyes to recognize you.*

May you, Lord God,

> *bring down the proud and outmaneuver the cunning;*
>> *raise the humble, and trip up the arrogant.*

Hold in your hand every circumstance of life,

> *whether we be rich or poor,*
>
> *whether we live or die,*
>
> *whether we discern every spirit, good or evil,*
>> *and the thoughts and intentions of every person.*

If we find ourselves in danger,

> *remind us that you come to our aid.*

When desperate,

> *you save us from a sense of failure.*

If events in the world threaten us,

> *we remember that you are the creator and guide of every living thing.*

Amen.

ST. CLEMENT OF ROME, FIRST CENTURY, ADAPTED

REMEMBER The creator and guide of every living thing has resources we barely dream about.

NOT SHUFFLING THROUGH LIFE

When things go well, we may, in all of our exuberance (or relief), forget the *why* of our happy circumstance. "When you drink from the stream," goes a Chinese proverb, "remember the spring." In C. S. Lewis's memorable image, we let our mind race up the sunbeam to the sun itself. Take a moment now and look around. Let your eye fasten on someone or something for which you are grateful. Let a prayer of gratitude form in your heart. Carry it with you on the tip of your tongue through the day.

PRAY

Lord, I want to praise you and delight in you,
*   not shuffle through life grudgingly.*
I want to be alert not only to this day's gifts
*   but also to you, the giver of gifts.*
Let my enjoyment of your world
*   only make me more conscious of your goodness.*
Let me be unstinting in my appreciation for your faithfulness
*   and confident that you can be trusted for everything.*
Amen.

REMEMBER When you drink from the stream, remember the springs from which it flows.

THE RIGHT TURN

It is hard to know which path to take some days. Our work-places, our friends, our entertainment media entice us with opportunities that, while not right, seem attractive neverthe-less, at least at first glance. They call us onto side trails or pull us off the way of faith altogether.

PRAY

O God, from whom to be turned is to fall,
  to whom to be turned is to rise,
    and with whom to stand is to abide forever,
Grant us in all our duties your help,
  in all our perplexities your guidance,
  in all our dangers your protection,
  and in all our sorrows your peace,
Through Jesus Christ our Lord.

ST. AUGUSTINE, FOURTH/FIFTH CENTURY

REMEMBER Walking with faith requires determination on our part and enabling grace on God's.

THE NARROW SELF

Many are the voices in our culture that would convince us that we can and should live for ourselves. "No one will look after you if you don't" becomes the hollow motto. Self-centeredness is justified, assumed. Even spirituality becomes an exercise in self-indulgence, little more than frenetic attempts to relieve the soul's hankering after warm feelings. But Jesus said, "Those who find their life will lose it, and those who lose their life for my sake will find it" (Matthew 10:39). How can you today give thought to an immense God who not only made us but also wants from us an offering of our whole heart, our entire lives?

PRAY

Teach me, my God and King,
In all things Thee to see
And in what I do in anything,
to do it as for Thee.
GEORGE HERBERT, SEVENTEENTH CENTURY

REMEMBER "A person wrapped up in himself or herself makes a very small bundle" (Benjamin Franklin, eighteenth century).

KINGDOM COME

A speaker once asked a group of college students a question for discussion: "What would you do if guaranteed absolute success at whatever you tried?" The answers were typical: make an ailing parent well, find the right partner to marry. One woman, though, shared an answer that made everyone laugh.

"I would bring in the kingdom of God," she said. In the quiet that fell after the laughter, she protested, "Why not? Why settle for less?"

Whatever we make of her youthful idealism, something in us longs for the coming reign of the God who continually works to bring into reality his purposes and plans.

PRAY

Lord, may your kingdom come. May your rule over the hearts of people produce great blessing and the spread of peace. May your kingdom's advance begin with me—within me. Amen.

REMEMBER In what specific way can you pray that God's kingdom—God's glorious reign—would come into being in your everyday arenas of work and love and service to others?

SPRING

WHEN RENEWAL FINALLY COMES

After winter's dark and cold, spring gently awakens earth with new growth. A similar seasonal rhythm undergirds our spiritual lives. We may have to wait for spring's renewing warmth, but it comes. It always comes.

PRAY

God of life and love, come to my hibernating heart. Nudge me awake that I might join creation in singing of your glories. You hold the earth and all of its seasons in your hand. And one day you will come again to usher in a final, joyous springtime of creation. In the meantime, let me never flag in knowing that you keep all of my life in your loving, watchful sight. In the name of Jesus. Amen.

REMEMBER "Be patient, therefore, beloved, until the coming of the Lord. The farmer waits for the precious crop from the earth, being patient with it until it receives the early and the late rains. You also must be patient. Strengthen your hearts, for the coming of the Lord is near" (James 5:7–8).

TO TURN TO GOD

We not only think about God, we *turn* toward God. We offer God our lives. We open our hearts to his indwelling presence. And that makes all the difference.

PRAY

Now we turn to the Lord God, the Father Almighty,
    and with pure hearts offer to him,
    so far as our littleness can,
    great and true thanks.
With all our hearts we pray for his surpassing kindness,
    that of his good pleasure he would hear our prayers,
    that by his power he would drive out the enemy
        from our deeds and thoughts,
    that he would increase our faith,
    guide our understandings,
    give us spiritual thoughts,
    and lead us to his deep joy,
through Jesus Christ His Son our Lord,
    who lives and reigns with him,
    in the unity of the Holy Spirit,
    one God, for ever and ever. Amen.

ST. AUGUSTINE, FOURTH/FIFTH CENTURY

REMEMBER Make it a point today to orient your life and your choices and your thoughts around the One who waits for your approach.

THE HOPE OF THOSE WHO CRY OUT

Sometimes all God needs to move into a situation or circumstance is a simple invitation from us.

PRAY

Lord, our God, great, eternal, wonderful in glory,
who keeps covenant and his promises
for the ones who love you with their whole heart,
who is the Life of all,
the help of those who run to you,
the hope of those who cry out for you,
cleanse us from our sins, secret and open,
and from every thought displeasing to you in your goodness.
Cleanse our bodies and souls,
our hearts and our consciences,
that with a pure heart and a clear soul,
with complete love and a calm hope,
we may venture confidently and fearlessly
into times of prayer to you. Amen.
COPTIC LITURGY OF ST. BASIL, ADAPTED

REMEMBER "God often visits us, but we are usually not home" (Polish proverb).

BETWEEN THE DREAMING
AND THE DOING

Sometimes our lives lack luster or inspiration because we do not fix our eyes on what can be, on whom we can more truly be like. We settle for puny heroes and dubious role models. Why not think today about Jesus—not only who he was, but also how he lived? Let his example become for you an invitation to do as he did, to love as he loved, and to grow in depending on God as Jesus daily depended on God.

PRAY

Dear Jesus, in whose life I see
All that I would, but fail to be,
Let your clear light forever shine,
To inspire and guide this life of mine.

Though what I dream and what I do
In my weak days are always two,
Help me, oppressed by things undone,
O you whose deeds and dreams were one!
JOHN HUNTER, EIGHTEENTH CENTURY, ADAPTED

REMEMBER Jesus not only loves us, he models for us life as it can be and invites us to follow the way he blazes before us.

A PRAYER FOR MERCY

Intentions have a place, but God finds the mettle of what we say we will do in what we actually attempt. God will not demand perfection, but he does expect authenticity.

PRAY

Almighty God, Father of mercies,
may you bring about and fashion in me
    what you have commanded should be in me.
Give me, O Lord, the grace of an authentic sorrow for wrong:
    turn my sin into heartfelt regret,
    let my regret move into forgiveness,
    and teach me to carefully watch over my behavior
        so that I do not violate your holy laws willfully.
May it become the work of my life to obey you,
    the joy of my soul to please you,
    and the culmination of my desires to live with you
        in the kingdom of your grace and glory. Amen.

JEREMY TAYLOR, SEVENTEENTH CENTURY, ADAPTED

REMEMBER Pray throughout today for an authentic faith.

THE HUMAN BATTLEFIELD

"The devil wrestles with God," said Russian novelist Fyodor Dostoyevsky, "and the battlefield is the human heart." The Bible tells us not only that evil exists but also that it works with persuasive and intensely personal power. Biblical writers saw the devil (so often the butt of our jokes) as more than a symbol of our dark side, more than a metaphor. Evil arises from within us, but we also experience it as a force outside of us.

Perhaps on your job today you will encounter powerful evil—in the mechanisms of the workplace, in another person fleeing from good (and God), and even within yourself.

PRAY

Remind me, Lord, that even though evil may seem pervasive at times, it ultimately will not win the battle. Through Christ, you have, as the apostle Paul wrote, "disarmed the rulers and authorities and made a public example of them, triumphing over them in it" (Colossians 2:15).

REMEMBER "The devil cannot hold sway over those who serve God with their whole hearts and who place their hope in God. The devil can wrestle with but not overcome them" (Shepherd of Hermas, second century, adapted).

THE SOUL'S DARK NIGHT

Sometimes, to our surprise, we find ourselves enduring what St. John of the Cross called a dark night of the soul. God may seem far off and bright days a distant memory. Such experiences may at some time visit all who follow God. "God leads into the dark night the people he wants to purify from all imperfections. In this way God can bring them farther along. When they . . . believe that the sun of divine favor shines most brightly upon them, God turns this light into darkness. . . . For God now sees that they have grown a little, and are becoming strong enough to lay aside their infants' clothes and be taken from the gentle breast. So God sets them down from his arms and teaches them to walk on their own feet" (St. John of the Cross, sixteenth century, adapted).

Fortunately, through these times God may show us more profound lessons about who he is. If we do not give up, through the shadows we will discover that God sees us and promises never to leave us stranded.

PRAY

Lord, your wisest sages remind me that I cannot expect the life of faith to be always celestial fireworks and warmhearted ecstasies. Easter comes only after the cross. Help me not flinch from difficulty or from times when your presence seems less real. Through Jesus, who endured rejection and suffering and death for us— for me. Amen.

REMEMBER God leads us into dark nights in order to bring us further along our journey of faith.

THE GREAT THIRST

A friend confessed of her and her husband's career track, "I used to believe that when we moved up the corporate ladder, when we made more money, when we bought a bigger house, *then* we'd be happy. I'm beginning to see that's not true. You only want more—and are still not satisfied." She was discovering that the aftertaste of affluence is not always sweet. More is needed to quench our thirst for meaning and divine connection.

PRAY

As a deer yearns
>*for running streams,*
so I yearn
>*for you, my God.*
I thirst for God,
>*the living God;*
when shall I go to see
>*the face of God? ...*
Why be so downcast,
>*why all these sighs?*
Hope in God! I will praise him still,
>*my Saviour, my God.*

PSALM 42:1–2, 5–6, NJB

REMEMBER God can help you find your true satisfaction.

THROUGH EVERY CHANGING STATE

Sometimes we get the idea that a mature spiritual life should exempt us from emotional ups and downs. But for most of us, times of dullness, even occasional depression, alternate with high moments and daily ecstasies. Ups and downs on a hospital monitor, after all, represent a beating heart; a flat line means you're dead! We do well to remember that fluctuations are part of any life—working, relating to colleagues and family, coping with daily demands. Invite God now into your emotional life.

PRAY

Lord, you have made me, and you know me well.
You see me and draw near beside me at all times.
May your presence give joy when I am dejected.
> *Peace when afraid.*
>> *Confidence when disturbed.*
>>> *Steady calmness when exhilarated.*
Remind me that you, O Lord, are with me
> *through every inner movement,*
>> *every changing state.*
You can be depended on no matter what I think or fear or feel or do.
Through the One whom the Bible calls the same
> *yesterday, today, and forever. Amen.*

REMEMBER Whatever you are feeling—the pleasure of accomplishment, the anxiety over rumored layoffs, the sadness of a friend's loss—allow God to be your companion.

DOUBTING

Because the Bible and many religious traditions place so much accent on believing, we are liable to worry when we wrestle with doubt. But doubt can be simply one aspect of growing closer to God. It doesn't need to paralyze us or make us fear that we are losing our standing with God. "Christ never failed to distinguish between doubt and unbelief. Doubt is can't believe; unbelief is won't believe. Doubt is honesty; unbelief is obstinacy. Doubt is looking for light; unbelief is content with darkness" (John Drummond, nineteenth century).

PRAY

You've brought me through so many times before. Let me believe in you. Sometimes my faith in you is so real; I have confidence you'll guide me on the right path. Then I doubt, and nothing seems possible. Let me see you working in my life. If you are breaking me down so that something else can be built up, please be gentle with me.[9]

PAUL WILKES

REMEMBER As much as you are able today, gently turn your doubting thoughts into questions addressed to God. Let them be occasions for exploring more deeply what you know—and don't know—about God.

THE LURE OF FALSE GODS

How long, O [people], will you turn my glory into shame?
How long will you love delusions and seek false gods?
PSALM 4:2, NIV

PRAY

*Lord, I am not tempted to worship idols made of stone. But I
confess that I do fight the pull to seek the gods of fame and for-
tune and productivity. Here at work I sometimes forget why I am
here. I get caught up, preoccupied, driven. I need your help, O
God, in keeping you at the center of my affections and ambitions. I want to live by faith, not by adrenaline. And I want to
serve, not just produce. Remind me of Jesus, who never forgot
whose he was. In whose name I pray. Amen.*

REMEMBER "For most of us, the great danger is not that we will
renounce our faith. It is that we will become so distracted and
rushed and preoccupied that we will settle for a mediocre
version of it" (John Ortberg).[10]

A SACRED GARDEN

More than one wise teacher has likened tending our spiritual growth to the work of a farmer or gardener. We have much to do to make the life of goodness take deeper root, as one guide realized:

The beginner must realize that in order to delight the Lord he is about to cultivate a garden on barren soil, full of weeds. His Majesty uproots the weeds and will set good plants in their stead. . . . Like good gardeners we must now, by God's help, make these plants grow, and to water them carefully, so that they do not wither but may produce flowers that will give off a pleasant fragrance to provide refreshment to this Lord of ours, so that he may often come into the garden to take his pleasure and have his delight among these virtues.

TERESA OF ÁVILA, SIXTEENTH CENTURY, ADAPTED

PRAY

Lord, I want to tend carefully the growing life
*   you are planting in me.*
Give me diligence and willingness
*   to continue to grow and flourish.*
Through Jesus I pray. Amen.

REMEMBER Living faithfully on the job, in our homes, and anywhere we find ourselves requires cultivation.

BABY STEPS

Sometimes we discount the small and incremental. But when it comes to our soul's growth and our deepening intimacy with God, we should not underestimate small steps. A conscience awakens to a small act of compromise usually glossed over, a heart feels a stirring for God's presence, someone decides to leaf through the Bible instead of *People* magazine—these are the steps that lead somewhere.

PRAY

Come in much mercy, O Lord, down into my soul and take possession and live there. A plain home, I confess, for so glorious a Majesty, but you nevertheless are readying it to receive yourself, through the desires you inspire in me. Enter, then, and beautify it, and make it such that you can indeed live there, since it is the work of your hands. Give me your own self, without which, though you would give me all that you have made, yet could not satisfy my desires. Let my soul always seek you, and let me persist in seeking, until I find, and am in full possession of you.
ST. AUGUSTINE, FOURTH/FIFTH CENTURY, ADAPTED

REMEMBER "Do not be afraid of growing slowly; be afraid only of standing still" (Chinese proverb).

HUMBLE PIE

We're not likely to think positively of the word *humility*. It even sounds like its unpleasant lexical cousin: *humiliation*. But humility, that blessed ability not to think more highly of ourselves than we ought, actually carries great benefits to the mind and soul. And to our surprise, we will actually find great freedom in not having always to be at the center of attention or on top of the heap.

PRAY

Lord, I want to make room for you in humility. Allow me to discover sooner rather than later the weariness of living always for myself. Give me motivating glimpses of the joys that come to those who put their focus outside themselves, especially above themselves.

REMEMBER "There is nothing more precious to God, or more profitable to humankind, than humble obedience. In God's eyes, one good work, wrought from true obedience, is of more value than a hundred thousand, wrought from self-will, contrary to obedience" (*Theologia Germanica,* fourteenth century).

PRIDE'S PERILS

Pride, one of the so-called seven deadly sins, often trips us up in subtle ways. Pride is not so much being proud of an accomplishment as being self-absorbed. Arrogance qualifies as a form of pride, obviously, but then so does a self-pitying, victim mentality. In both attitudes we immerse ourselves in the self. Is pride afflicting you in any way today?

PRAY

Lord, it is easy to become preoccupied with myself. I pray that you grab my attention so that I become fascinated and awed by you. As I ponder your greatness and goodness, allow my focus on self gradually to give way to openness to you and compassion for others. Amen.

REMEMBER "Like some pestilential disease, [pride] attacks the whole person, and not content to damage one part or one limb only, it injures the entire body by its deadly influence, and endeavors to throw down . . . and destroy those who were already at the top of the tree of the virtues" (St. John Cassian, fourth/fifth century).

A TENDER, COSTLY LOVE

Few symbols convey such power and meaning as the cross. What Jesus did there reminds us that we owe our life to the death of another. We find peace in the battle waged on our behalf. We become more fully ourselves by walking in Jesus' steps as he makes his way to his suffering.

PRAY

Almighty and everliving God,

    in your tender love for the human race

        you sent your Son our Savior Jesus Christ

           to take upon him our human nature,

               and to suffer death upon the cross,

               giving us the example of his great humility.

Mercifully grant that we may walk in the way of his suffering,

    and also share in his resurrection;

through Jesus Christ our Lord,

        who lives and reigns with you and the Holy Spirit,

           one God, for ever and ever. Amen.

THE BOOK OF COMMON PRAYER

REMEMBER "Therefore, since we are justified by faith, we have peace with God through our Lord Jesus Christ" (Romans 5:1).

WHEN HE SUFFERED

When [Jesus] was abused, he did not return abuse; when he suffered, he did not threaten; but he entrusted himself to the one who judges justly. He himself bore our sins in his body on the cross, so that, free from sins, we might live for righteousness; by his wounds you have been healed.

1 PETER 2:23–24

PRAY

Lord, teach us to understand that your Son died
to save us not from suffering
but from ourselves,
not from injustice, far less from justice,
but from being unjust.
He died that we might live—
as he lives,
by dying as he died
who died to himself.

GEORGE MACDONALD, NINETEENTH CENTURY

REMEMBER God offers us a profoundly new life through the death of his Son.

OVERCOMING THE IMAGES OF EVIL

Sometimes the images thrust upon us from movies and TV advertisements accent gloom and violence. Portrayals of villains in entertainment media often carry more impact and immediacy than do the models of the good and decent. The result can be a dreary, disheartening picture of the world.

Religious faith has always accented images and language and stories full of vivid confirmation that the good will prevail. Perhaps no story better demonstrates this than the Bible's graphic depiction of Jesus' death and resurrection.

PRAY

We thank you, heavenly Father, that you have delivered us from the dominion of sin and death and brought us into the kingdom of your Son; and we pray that, as by his death he has recalled us to life, so by his love he may raise us to eternal joys; who lives and reigns with you, in the unity of the Holy Spirit, one God, now and for ever. Amen.

THE BOOK OF COMMON PRAYER

REMEMBER Whatever season of the year (or of life) you find yourself in, the Easter message of a victorious Savior can carry you through the day and remind you that all will turn out right, no matter how discouraging the world appears.

WHERE LOVE COMES FROM

As for that which is beyond your strength, be absolutely certain that our Lord loves you, devotedly and individually, loves you. . . . Give yourself up with joy to a loving confidence in God.
ABBE HENRI DE TOURVILLE, NINETEENTH CENTURY

PRAY

Lord, grant me
I pray in the name of Jesus Christ the Son, my Lord,
   that love that knows no end
      so that my lamp may feel your kindling touch
       and know no quenching.
May it burn for me
   and for others give light.
ST. COLUMBANUS, SIXTH/SEVENTH CENTURY, ADAPTED

REMEMBER "If we have got the true love of God shed abroad in our hearts, we will show it in our lives. We will not have to go up and down the earth proclaiming it. We will show it in everything we say and do" (D. L. Moody, nineteenth century).

HOW THE EVERYDAY MATTERS MUCH

Sometimes it seems that we plod along, not seeing much good result from our good intentions, not realizing the successes we hoped for, not winning the world's praise and admiration. Day in and day out, what we do seems so simple, small, and *ordinary*. But we miss a powerful truth if we take all that to mean that our lives do not matter. Great good lies hidden in our smallest deeds, our quietest gestures, and our least-noticed efforts—more good than we can realize.

PRAY

Lord, help me see how my life's everyday acts can be pleasing to you and a godsend to others. Keep me from assuming that those who create a big splash and work under the public eye are the only ones who change the face of the world. Amen.

REMEMBER "[May you] lead lives worthy of the Lord, fully pleasing to him, as you bear fruit in every good work and as you grow in the knowledge of God" (Colossians 1:10).

A GOOD RETURN

We may picture making ourselves available to God as impossibly complicated, beyond our will or expertise. But we need not have arrived in order to begin. We start simply, where we are. We notice a simple stirring, a quiet longing. We pay attention to it. And then we tell God that we are ready, that we are willing—and willing to be made more willing.

PRAY

Take, Lord, and receive all my liberty,
my memory, my understanding,
and all my will.
All that I have you gave to me:
to you, Lord, I return it!
All that I have you gave to me:
use it according to your will.
Give me your love and grace,
for this will be enough for me.

ST. IGNATIUS OF LOYOLA, SIXTEENTH CENTURY, ADAPTED

REMEMBER To submit our lives to God is to place them in the hands of a gentle power and strong presence. We never do more to achieve our potential as when we yield ourselves to One who can do far more with us than we can do ourselves.

RECOVERING WONDER

Many of us, after living a while and seeing a lot, become a bit bored, even jaded. When that happens, we stop expecting much, resigning ourselves to life pretty much as it is. The missing dimension is wonder, a sense of the marvel of life. But it's never too late to recover a new sense of wonder. It's never too late to ask God for it.

PRAY

Lord, keep me from an "I've been this way before" or "I know this already" attitude. Revive in me a new awareness that you are alive and awake in the world and therefore every day can be filled with good things, even surprises.

REMEMBER "How many common things are trodden underfoot which, if examined carefully, awaken our astonishment" (St. Augustine, fourth/fifth century).

FORGETTING WHO'S WHO

It is clear that not our diligence, but the providence of God, even where we seem to be active, effects everything that happens. So that, were God to forsake us, no care, nor anxiety, nor toil, nor any other such thing, will ever appear to come to anything, but all will utterly pass away.

ST. JOHN CHRYSOSTOM, HOMILY 21, FOURTH CENTURY

PRAY

Powerful God, sometimes I forget that you are wonderfully working out your plans in what happens. Even in what I think I do, you are at work, you are the One who ultimately can bring accomplishment. And without you, what could I do? I offer myself to you anew, O Lord, inviting you to make use of me in whatever ways you see fit. Amen.

REMEMBER Jesus said, "I am the vine, you are the branches. Whoever remains in me, with me in him, bears fruit in plenty; for cut off from me you can do nothing" (John 15:5, NJB).

GOD BEYOND KNOWING

Oh, the depth of the riches of the wisdom and knowledge
of God!

How unsearchable his judgments,
and his paths beyond tracing out!

"Who has known the mind of the Lord?
Or who has been his counselor?"

"Who has ever given to God,
that God should repay him?"

ROMANS 11:33–35, NIV

PRAY

*O God, whom Scripture says is alone immortal and who lives in
unapproachable light, whom no one has seen or can see, keep us
from thinking we can manage you or too neatly define you. Give
us an adventurous awe and a delighted sense of wonder, that we
not forget how great and beyond knowing you are. In Jesus'
name. Amen.*

REMEMBER "We only know God truly when we believe that God
is far beyond all that we can possibly think of God" (St.
Thomas Aquinas, thirteenth century).

A STUBBORN LOVE

What unparalleled condescension and divinely tender mercies are displayed [by God]! Did the judge ever beseech a condemned criminal to accept of pardon? Does the creditor ever beseech a ruined debtor to receive an acquittance in full? Yet our almighty Lord, and our eternal Judge, not only kindly grants to offer these blessings, but invites us, entreats us, and, with the most tender persistence, solicits us not to reject them.

JOHN WESLEY, EIGHTEENTH CENTURY

PRAY

Lord, keep me from disregarding the gracious provision in your divine love. May it become more and more my help and hope. I can get full of myself and empty of grace, but you always call me back, and you receive me with open arms, ready and able to help me move on. Amen.

REMEMBER Sometimes we forget just how valuable forgiveness is. Or we grow oblivious to our need for it. But when we do realize our immersion in self, our indifference to others, or our wild efforts to keep God at arm's length, forgiveness comes to mean so much!

A JOURNEY OF MERCIES

We find it easy to nurse our worries, of course; that's become something of a national pastime. But we have a Person to whom to take them—and with whom we can leave them.

PRAY

Dear God, my whole life has been a journey of mercies and blessings shown to one most undeserving of them. Year after year you have carried me on, removed dangers from my path, refreshed me, been patient with me, directed me, sustained me. Do not leave me when my strength fails me. And you never will forsake me. I can rest securely on you. As I am true to your ways, you will, to the very end, be superabundantly good to me. I may rest upon your arm; I may go to sleep in you bosom.

JOHN HENRY NEWMAN, NINETEENTH CENTURY

REMEMBER "Let us be like a bird for a moment perched / On a frail branch when he sings; / Though he feels it bend, yet he sings his song, / Knowing that he has wings" (Victor Hugo, nineteenth century).

WHAT ONLY GOD CAN GIVE

We doubt the truth of it much of the time, but God reminds us through Jesus' life and death and resurrection that we can always come to God. God's promise to receive us is a gracious, standing invitation.

PRAY

It is so hard for me to believe fully in the love that flows from your heart. I am so insecure, so fearful, so doubtful and so distrustful. While I say with my words that I believe in your full and unconditional love, I continue to look for affection, support, acceptance and praise among my fellow human beings, always expecting from them what only you can give.

I clearly hear your voice saying, "Come to me you who labor and are overburdened ... for I am gentle and humble in heart," and yet I run off in other directions as if I did not trust you.... O Lord, why is it that I am so eager to receive human praise and human support even when experience tells me how limited and conditional is the love that comes from a human heart?[11]

HENRI NOUWEN

REMEMBER Often our insecurities have nothing to do with our circumstances and everything to do with our forgetting divine grace.

THE ONLY TRUE REMEDY

Sometimes a feeling of unworthiness drives us to prayer. We keenly sense our need for forgiveness and a new beginning, and we turn naturally to God. This process can happen anywhere—including our workplace. Our jobs and relationships and other circumstances actually present us with daily reminders of our faults and failings. At such times, prayer for help is a valid—and vitally important—response.

"When any for relief run to confess [their shortcomings], the only true remedy for them is prayer; to present themselves before God as criminals, beg strength of him to rise out of this state. Then they will soon be changed, and brought out of the mire and clay" (Madame Guyon, seventeenth/eighteenth century).

PRAY

Have mercy on me, O God,
*   according to your steadfast love....*
Wash me thoroughly from my iniquity,
*   and cleanse me from my sin.*
For I know my transgressions....
Create in me a clean heart, O God,
*   and put a new and right spirit within me.*

PSALM 51:1–3, 10

REMEMBER We need not be elaborate or long-winded as we seek help, just willing to ask.

SINKING IN DEEP MIRE

If you should temporarily lose your sense of well-being, don't be too quick to despair. With humility and patience, wait for God who is able to give you back even more comfort. There is nothing novel about this to those who are familiar with God's ways. The great saints and ancient prophets frequently experienced this alternation of up and down, joy and sorrow.

THOMAS À KEMPIS, FOURTEENTH/FIFTEENTH CENTURY

PRAY

Save me, O God; for the waters are come in to my soul.
I sink in deep mire, where there is no standing.
I am come into deep waters,
  where the floods overflow me.
I am weary of my crying: my throat is dried.
My eyes fail while I wait for my God.

PSALM 69:1–3, KJV, ADAPTED

REMEMBER Let today have moments of waiting, times of opening to God's next offer of help.

ASKING GOD TO HURRY

Examples of prayer in the Bible are sometimes surprising. Scripture's models of a spiritual life do not always fit our neatly laid out models. Many of the people God favored had a frankness in prayer that can be startling. Are there ways in which you are holding back because you're afraid that God won't "take it"? Are there urgencies in your life that would lead you to cry out if you were confident that was okay? Spend some time today allowing your requests to blurt out with new boldness.

PRAY

Make haste, O God, to deliver me;
*   make haste to help me, O LORD. . . .*
Let all those that seek you rejoice and be glad in you.
Let such as love your salvation say continually,
"Let God be magnified."
But I am poor and needy.
Make haste for me, O God.
You are my help and my deliverer; O LORD,
*   do not dawdle.*

PSALM 70:1, 4–5, KJV, ADAPTED

REMEMBER "To God we use the simplest, shortest words we can find because eloquence is only air and noise to him" (F. W. Robertson, nineteenth century).

HARD-WON SILENCE

"Silence is golden," we say. "How I would love some peace and quiet," we mutter. But it may not be so simple to get or—once we have it—to enjoy. Turn off all the outer racket and still we hear a kind of inner noise. Our worries, fears, and jealousies clamor with loud and distracting voices.

As you attempt to carve out a few moments today for quiet reflection, don't be surprised if your mind stays active. Turn your concerns into prayers. And don't let the distractions keep you from keeping on!

PRAY

Lord, your prophet Isaiah tells us
    that in returning and rest is our salvation,
    in quietness and trust is our strength.
Help us long for silence,
    and finding a few quiet moments,
        persevere in it,
    that our lives will not be nonstop talk and sound,
        but filled with pauses for reflection on you. Amen.

REMEMBER In returning and rest is our salvation.

DON'T FORGET!

At a time when many people are rediscovering the value of traditions and roots, it may not surprise us to learn that remembering is also a kind of spiritual discipline. In passage after passage of the Bible and in great spiritual teachings, we find the summons to remember what God has done. Our memories keep us going when all does not seem to be what we think it should be. Recalling actions or aspects of God can keep us from losing hope.

PRAY

I will remember the works of the LORD;
   surely I will remember your wonders of old.
I will meditate also on all your work, and talk of your doings.
Your way, O God, is in the sanctuary;
   who is so great a God as our God?
You are the God that does wonders.
You have declared your strength among the people.
You have with your arm redeemed your people.

PSALM 77:11–15, KJV, ADAPTED

REMEMBER "Memory is the cabinet of imagination, the treasury of reason, the registry of conscience, and the council chamber of thought" (St. Basil, fourth century).

DEALING WITH THE DARK IMPULSES AND DAILY SINS

While charging through our too-busy, unreflected-on life, we may forget our shortcomings and dark impulses. We may overlook or ignore their corrosive, subtle effects. We may neglect to seek cleansing release. It is no morbid enterprise to consider our misdeeds, only the better part of wisdom. And it is necessary if we are to move forward.

PRAY

O Lord, give us ... we implore you, grace and strength to overcome every sin: sins that attach themselves and attack us, sins we plan, sins that catch us by surprise, sins of negligence and omission, sins against you, ourself, our neighbor, sins great, small, remembered, forgotten. Amen.

CHRISTINA ROSSETTI, NINETEENTH CENTURY, ADAPTED

REMEMBER "It is necessary to repent for years in order to erase a fault in the eyes of people; a single tear suffices with God" (François-Auguste-René de Chateaubriand, eighteenth/nineteenth century).

THE POWER OF A GRUDGE

It is the rare workplace that knows no tense words or hurt feelings. Perhaps you work with someone who tries your patience or with whom you can barely (or not at all) relate. Maybe someone has wronged you and left you furious or demolished. Why not bring that situation to God in prayer?

PRAY

God of love, who has given through your only Son a new commandment to love one another, even as you loved us, the unworthy and the wandering, and gave your beloved Son for our life and salvation, we pray you, Lord, to give to us your servants, in all our time on earth, a mind forgetful of past ill will, a pure conscience, and a heart to love our sisters and brothers. Amen.
COPTIC LITURGY OF ST. CYRIL

REMEMBER "For the sake of one good action a hundred evil ones should be forgotten" (Chinese proverb).

"We pardon to the degree that we love" (François de La Rochefoucauld, seventeenth century).

THE TRUTH WE LONG FOR

Because of our culture's current penchant for tolerance, honesty may become a casualty when we feel pressure from colleagues. What used to be called "the hard truth" somehow gets translated into a soft suggestion. Today consider if there are ways you hedge on saying what really needs to be said. Reflect on ways you have allowed subtle falsehoods to infiltrate your attitudes or words. Perhaps you need to be bolder with those you work with, or more honest with yourself.

Because God is true, there is great strength in our being truthful. When we resist the temptation to fudge—even in little ways—we live by an aspect of God's very character.

PRAY

O God, You Who are the truth, make me one with You in love everlasting. I am often wearied by the many things I hear and read, but in You is all that I long for.

THOMAS À KEMPIS, FOURTEENTH/FIFTEENTH CENTURY

REMEMBER By being truthful, we demonstrate our conviction that truth is more powerful than deception. We align our little lives with the truth that will triumph in the end.

NOT GIVING UP IN PRAYER

When we are in trouble, [God] will have us to pray; for God often seems to hide himself, and will not hear or allow himself to be found. Then we must seek him, continuing in prayer. When we seek him, he often locks himself up, as it were, in a private chamber; if we intend to come in unto him, then we must knock and when we have knocked once or twice, then he appears to hear a little. At last, when we keep on knocking, he opens the door and says, "What will you have?" We say, "Lord, we would have this or that." And then he says, "Take it and have it." In just this way must we persist in praying, and wake God up.

MARTIN LUTHER, FIFTEENTH/SIXTEENTH CENTURY

PRAY

Lord, let my prayers this day not be faint or halfhearted. Help me pray with all of my being and not forget to seek your help often and persistently.

REMEMBER "Ask and it will be given to you; seek and you will find; knock and the door will be opened to you" (Matthew 7:7, NIV).

A WISH TURNED GODWARD

Prayer presents us with opportunities to remember others and their sometimes desperate situations. The Bible frequently urges us to intercessory prayer, that is, prayer for and on behalf of others. Jesus certainly encouraged this: Ask, seek, knock, he said. The apostle Paul told some first-century Christians, "In all your prayer and entreaty keep praying in the Spirit on every possible occasion. Never get tired of staying awake to pray for all God's holy people" (Ephesians 6:18, NJB).

Recall today one or two people who could benefit from your remembering them in prayer.

PRAY

Lord, in ways I can't fully understand, you have enlisted me to do your work and share in your purposes. Hear my prayer now for those you bring to my mind. May I not be callused or indifferent to the good my prayers for them may accomplish. In Jesus' name. Amen.

REMEMBER "A prayer in its simplest definition is merely a wish turned Godward" (Phillips Brooks, nineteenth century).

WHEN WE CAN'T SEEM TO PRAY ENOUGH

Sometimes when we have been lax in praying, consumed by tasks that seem to leave us no room for reflection on God, we come back to prayer with a sense of having missed a great deal or messed up completely. The thing to do is not to waste energy berating ourselves but simply to confess to God our lack of attentiveness, receive his forgiveness, and quickly turn our hearts and minds back to him.

PRAY

Gracious Father, ever ready to have your children return home to your side, hear my prayers. I want to pray, and I want to pray more. Let my regrets not keep me from coming, once I do remember to turn my heart toward you. And when I come, let me find greater and greater joy in you. Through Jesus I pray. Amen.

REMEMBER "Do not forget to pray. Every time you pray, if your prayer is heartfelt, there will be new feeling and new meaning to it, which will give you fresh courage, and you will understand that prayer is an education" (Fyodor Dostoyevsky, nineteenth century).

RUNNING IN THE PATH OF GOD'S WAYS

It is one thing to walk and run and scurry around. We may cover a lot of ground. But what if we are not going in the right direction? What if we fail to make true progress? Pause now and consider if your life is headed where it needs to be going.

PRAY

Lord, I do not want my life to move toward that which is false or fleeting.

May I find my way to what lasts.

Let my thoughts and affections take me to you.

"I run in the path of your commands," prayed the psalmist,

"for you have set my heart free" (Psalm 119:32, NIV).

May that become my prayer.

Amen.

REMEMBER "In all things, both high and low, let God be your goal" (St. John of the Cross, sixteenth century).[12]

PRAYING WITH A CLEAN SLATE

"Resentment casts a cloud over your prayers," said fourth-century teacher Evagrius Ponticus. As you pray today, perhaps your heart is testy or bitter toward someone you work with or live with. Perhaps you have grown indifferent to another's need.

PRAY

Gracious God, don't let my prayers make me distant from others,
but may they drive me deeper into others' lives.
Help me to learn from your generous heart
to be generous with others.
Help me to find in your unbelievably lavish forgiveness
the inspiration and power to forgive those who hurt or
offend me.
Amen.

REMEMBER Allow your prayer today to become an invitation to reconnect with God and with people rather than an opportunity to isolate yourself or retreat from others.

LIVING PRAYER

Prayer belongs in everyday life, not just exalted moments of worship. It should have a feel of ordinary life along with its high thoughts.

PRAY

Help me wake up to the wonder of the world you have made.
Help my eyes catch at least glimpses of the hidden beauties
of the day.
Help me stay alert to the ways you lead me.
Help me live fully in the face of the promises you give.

May your plans for us surprise us in our routines,
that we never take a day for granted.

REMEMBER "Certain thoughts are prayers. There are moments when, whatever be the attitude of the body, the soul is on its knees" (Victor Hugo, nineteenth century).

MORE THAN A "NICE" ACTIVITY

We may sometimes think of our praying as a pleasant pastime, yet ultimately innocuous. But when we do, we ignore the Bible's constant, rugged regard for the significance of our praying. Through prayer we do nothing less than participate with God in the working out of eternal purposes. Folding our hands in prayer does not mean we resign ourselves to fate but that we help unleash God's activity in the world.

PRAY

O righteous God,
    who searches minds and hearts,
  bring to an end the violence of the wicked
      and make the righteous secure.

PSALM 7:9, NIV

REMEMBER What need in the world tugs on your heart that can be turned into prayer this day—prayer you can say in your mind or under your breath, even as you go about your tasks?

GUARDING WORDS

How great a forest is set ablaze by a small fire! And the tongue is a fire.

JAMES 3:5–6

PRAY

Lord, may my words not be hurtful or flippant today.

Sometimes I forget how powerful the tongue is.

Or I ignore my conscience in favor of the delicious temptation to gossip.

How easy it is to let my words take on a life of their own,

a life that ultimately robs life from others

and that tears down and ravages.

Let me instead find ways to act and speak in love.

Amen.

REMEMBER "Let your speech be such that no one may be offended, and let it concern things that would not cause you regret were all to know of them" (St. John of the Cross, sixteenth century).[13]

THE GIFT OF AN EAR

Listening—truly listening—to the people we work with means more than cocking an ear for the sounds and syllables of speech. It means listening in a deeper way for what a person is feeling and experiencing. This kind of listening with the "third ear," as someone has called it, can allow us to be sensitive to currents that run under the words that people speak aloud. Cultivating such sensitivity can go a long way in creating a good atmosphere in our workplaces.

PRAY

Lord, help me be quick to listen, slow to speak. I want to be sensitive to what people around me need or think. I pray this in the name of Jesus, who showed himself able and willing to listen to people's profoundest longings, joys, and heartaches.

REMEMBER Many people need to be listened to. Often the best gift we can give is the quiet and space that invites them to open up and enables them to speak honestly from the heart.

LIVING—THIS INSTANT!

It is not easy to live in the present, being fully *present*. We are more liable to squirm in the grip of past mistakes, hurts, or heartaches. Or maybe we stew over the future's uncertain prospects. But the present is the only arena in which we can act; only now can we seize the day and live fully. No wonder French mystical writer Jean Pierre de Caussade spoke of the *sacrament* of the present moment. It is here, now, right where we are that we can open up to God, to others, and to what matters. This instant provides the opportunities that God will bless, if we will only recognize them.

PRAY

Lord, I want to focus on what is before me, not cringe over what has been or worry over what might be. Help me open myself to your forgiveness, which frees me from the past, and your hope, which allows me to relax about the future. Here am I. Amen.

REMEMBER "The right time for seeking God is always now" (St. Bernard of Clairvaux, twelfth century).

THE WAY GOD IS

Someone once said that the most interesting thing about religion is God. God is worthy of our fascination, not just our duties or routine prayers. When we praise God, we acknowledge him and adore him for his character. We can find great delight in remembering who God *is*, not simply what he does for us.

PRAY

Lord, sometimes I get caught up in the habits of my faith. I perform the actions without my heart being fully engaged in what I do. Or I look to you thinking only about what you can do, overlooking who you are. *Rebaptize my imagination with at least a glimpse of your unfathomable might and love, a new vision of your wonder and glory. Amen.*

REMEMBER "How rich and deep are the wisdom and the knowledge of God!" (Romans 11:33, NJB).

PRAYING THROUGH IT ALL

Prayer is more than a pleasant add-on; it is the way we live and breathe and move in God's very presence. Only through prayer can we become all God intends. Only as we make room for God do we experience our fullest selves and the richest possible life.

PRAY

Lord, circumstances today may get difficult. Things will happen that are beyond my control. I may get discouraged. Then again, things may take off, and I will feel that I own the world. Remind me through it all that prayer is at the heart of my relationship with you and at the root of any fruitful life. Turn me often toward you to pray in praise, longing, need, and hope. Remind me to include my colleagues and myself as the rest of today unfolds. Let my life become a prayer.

REMEMBER "Upright Christians pray without ceasing; though they pray not always with their mouths, yet their hearts pray continually, sleeping and waking; for the sigh of a true Christian is a prayer" (Martin Luther, fifteenth/sixteenth century).

THE SECRET OF CONTENTMENT

I know what it is to have little, and I know what it is to have plenty. In any and all circumstances I have learned the secret of being well-fed and of going hungry, of having plenty and of being in need. I can do all things through him who strengthens me.
PHILIPPIANS 4:12–13

PRAY

Almighty God, give to me, your follower, a tame and gentle spirit, that I may be slow to anger and quick to show mercy and forgiveness. Give me a wise and constant heart, that I may never be moved to an unchecked anger for any injury—attempted or accomplished. Lord, let me ever be courteous, and easily approached. Let me never fall into a catty or contentious spirit, but follow peace with all people, offering forgiveness, inviting them by kindnesses, ready to admit my own errors and make amends, and eager to be reconciled. Let no sickness or personal disappointment make me irritable or discontented or ungrateful, but in all things make me like the holy Jesus.
JEREMY TAYLOR, SEVENTEENTH CENTURY, ADAPTED

REMEMBER Strive to let nothing make you irritable or ungrateful today.

SIMPLICITY'S STARTING POINT

Those who want to lead a good life, said the medieval spiritual writer Meister Eckehart, should do as the person who wants to draw a perfect circle. First he or she fixes the sharp center point of the compass on the paper. Only then, Eckehart said, with the point in place, can an exact circle be drawn. Likewise, we are to fix our eyes and lives on God.

PRAY

Preserve us blameless, O Lord,
in our goings out and comings in this day.
Fill us with the simplicity of a divine purpose,
that we may be inwardly at one with your holy will,
and lifted above self-centered wishes of our own.
Set free from every detaining desire or reluctance,
may we heartily surrender all our powers
to the work that you have given us to do;
rejoicing in any toil,
and fainting under no hardness
that may befall us as good soldiers of Jesus Christ.
JAMES MARTINEAU, NINETEENTH CENTURY, ADAPTED

REMEMBER Start with the center point, not the periphery. Then the rest will follow.

MERCY FOR THOSE IN NEED

The workplace sometimes becomes a domain centered on itself. We forget how a wider world turns outside the confines of office rivalries or rumors of company shake-ups. Even when we feel called to throw ourselves into our jobs, we need to remember the needy—next door or around the globe. We pause to remember them, if just for a moment, and pray.

PRAY

Have mercy, O God, on all who sorrow,
  those who weep and those in exile.
Show kindness to the persecuted and the homeless
      who are without hope;
    those who are scattered in remote corners of this world;
      those imprisoned or ruled by dictators.
Have mercy on them as is written in your holy law,
  where your compassion is exalted!

JEWISH PRAYER

REMEMBER "I know that the LORD maintains the cause of the needy, and executes justice for the poor. Surely the righteous shall give thanks to your name; the upright shall live in your presence" (Psalm 140:12–13).

THE GLORY OF LITTLE THINGS

Do small things with great love.[14]
MOTHER TERESA OF CALCUTTA, TWENTIETH CENTURY

PRAY

Lord, I feel tempted to assign significance to the famous person and the public figure. Greatness seems reserved for the missionary or the priest or the political leader. But then you remind me that everything done for you carries weight. No one's life lacks importance, not when we can do deeds, offer gestures, and say words that bring kindness to others. Keep me from staying unimpressed by the small thing, but rather assist me to seize each opportunity, large or small, to do good and show love.

REMEMBER "Whoever can be trusted with very little can also be trusted with much" (Luke 16:10, NIV).

THE LIMITS OF DO-IT-YOURSELFISM

The lure of doing things ourselves is very strong. "Look, Mom, I'm doing it all by myself!" is the proud declaration of a child learning independence. As adults, too, we gain a supreme sense of accomplishment if we manage to finish something solo. It doesn't hurt, either, that by going it alone we avoid the risks (perhaps embarrassment) of asking for help. But does God intend it to be that way?

PRAY

Lord, rinse me clean of pride that makes me unwilling to turn to others for insight, support, affection, or guidance. I know that I need help with the perplexities of daily life. Let me seek and find those who can make my life stronger, richer, more centered.

REMEMBER "For where two or three are gathered in my name, I am there among them" (Jesus, in Matthew 18:20).

THE BEST THINGS ARE NEAREST

Anyone who has lived in farm country knows how ruler-straight and perfectly even plant rows can be in modern agriculture. Tilling a straight furrow requires keeping your eyes open and your gaze fixed on where you are headed. Think about some ways you may need to mind your rows today. Make sure you keep your eye on the goal that allows you to make your work straight.

PRAY

Lord, there are so many distractions that can pull my eyes off the most important tasks in front of me. Give me the ability to concentrate, to do my work, and to keep my responsibilities ordered and straight.

REMEMBER "The best things are nearest: breath in your nostrils, light in your eyes, flowers at your feet, duties at your hand, the path of God just before you. Then do not grasp at the stars, but do life's plain, common work as it comes" (Robert Louis Stevenson, nineteenth century).

WAKING UP MORE
THAN YOUR BODY

Awake, my soul, stretch every nerve,
And press with vigor on;
A heavenly race demands thy zeal,
And an immortal crown,
And an immortal crown.

A cloud of witnesses around
Hold thee in full survey;
Forget the steps already trod,
And onward urge thy way,
And onward urge thy way. . . .

Then wake, my soul, stretch every nerve,
And press with vigor on,
A heavenly race demands thy zeal,
And an immortal crown.

PHILIP DODDRIDGE, EIGHTEENTH CENTURY

PRAY

*Lord, help me to awake to you, to what matters, with every fiber
and cell of my being. Amen.*

REMEMBER "'Tis God's all animating voice / That calls thee
from on high; / 'Tis His own hand / Presents the prize / To
thine aspiring eye" (Philip Doddridge, eighteenth century).

WHAT MY SOUL REALLY WANTS

Self-help books and magazines sometimes suggest that we find ourselves by breaking free of commitment to others. They encourage us to get in touch with our own needs and wants and live for ourselves. But in doing so we settle for a false fulfillment. Such an approach to life will leave us hollowly alone and sick of self.

PRAY

Lord, help me find myself by finding you, by being found by you, by learning to live for a world outside myself. I don't want to end my life only to see that I have devoted myself to nothing higher or nobler than the gratification of my little needs. Help me catch a glimpse of your mighty goodness and pour out my life in response.

REMEMBER "My soul, wait only upon God; for my expectation is from him. . . . Trust in him at all times; everyone, pour out your heart before him: God is a refuge for us" (Psalm 62:5, 8, KJV, adapted).

THINK OF THE RAVENS

Think of the ravens. They do not sow or reap; they have no storehouses and no barns; yet God feeds them. And how much more you are worth than the birds! Can any of you, however much you worry, add a single cubit to your span of life? . . . Think how the flowers grow; they never have to spin or weave; yet, I assure you, not even Solomon in all his royal robes was clothed like one of them.

LUKE 12:24–27, NJB

PRAY

Almighty God, eternal treasure of all good things,
*   You fill everything with abundance.*
You clothe the lilies of the field and
*   feed the young ravens that call on you.*
Let your providence be my storehouse,
*   may the things I need form the basis of what I want.*
Never let my wants to grow out of greed,
*   my work to become all-important,*
*   or my concerns too heavy or distracting.*
Help me live in moderation,
*   holy, submitted to your will,*
*   willing to accept whatever you have planned for me.*

JEREMY TAYLOR, SEVENTEENTH CENTURY, ADAPTED

REMEMBER "Set your hearts on [God's] kingdom, and these other things will be given you as well" (Luke 12:31, NJB).

WHAT WE THINK WE WANT

So often we think that we know what we want! We are also convinced that we know precisely what to pray for: a promotion, a ticket to wealth, a certain turn in the road for a colleague or a loved one. But our vision is limited. Within a month we may thank God for not answering a certain prayer. And even when an "unanswered" prayer makes little sense, what else can we do but entrust the world's course to the God who made it and keeps it?

PRAY

We believe, O Lord, that we can trust the promise of him who said, ask and it will be given you, seek and you will find, knock and it will be opened unto you; and we in our wanting will pray for the things we need. We will bring an unflagging energy to the study of your prophets and apostles, and we will knock for entrance at every gate of hidden knowledge, but it is yours to answer the prayer, to grant the thing we seek, to open the door on which we beat.

ST. HILARY, FOURTH CENTURY

REMEMBER What seems like a "no" may be a "not yet." And whatever the answer or nonanswer, it may pave the way for a far better "yes."

A WIDE MERCY

There's a wideness in God's mercy,
Like the wideness of the sea;
There's a kindness in his justice,
Which is more than liberty.

But we make his love too narrow
By false limits of our own;
And we magnify his strictness
With a zeal he will not own.
FREDERICK WILLIAM FABER, NINETEENTH CENTURY

PRAY

Lord, today make me a grace-filled, gentler person. Give me the ability to look beyond others' faults, to ignore their barbed comments, to greet their indifference with genuine warmth. May I look out at the world of people today with a kind smile and with caring eyes, that others may at least begin to sense a goodness they may have forgotten exists. In the loving name of Jesus. Amen.

REMEMBER "But we make his love too narrow / By false limits of our own" (Frederick William Faber, nineteenth century).

DO WE WANT ENOUGH?

At times, we are like bundles of nonstop need and unsatisfied wants. We think we should curb our appetites and cravings. And sometimes we do, especially when they distract us with superficial or forbidden pleasures and leave us discontented.

But in another sense, we may not give our longings free-enough rein. Shouldn't our deepest longings lead ultimately to the One who alone gives rest to the restless soul?

PRAY

Look upon us, O Lord,
and let all the darkness of our souls
vanish before the beams of your brightness.
Fill us with holy love,
and open to us the treasures of your wisdom.
All our desire is known to you,
therefore perfect what you have begun,
and what your Spirit has awakened us to ask for in prayer.
We seek your face;
turn to us your face and show us your glory.
Then will our longing be satisfied,
and our peace will be complete.
ST. AUGUSTINE, FOURTH/FIFTH CENTURY, ADAPTED

REMEMBER This day, ask God for a holy longing and restlessness for him.

BE STILL AND KNOW

God is our refuge and strength,
    a very present help in trouble.
Therefore we will not fear, though the earth be removed,
    and though the mountains be carried into the sea;
Though its waters roar and be troubled,
    though the mountains shake with their swelling. . . .
The LORD of hosts is with us;
    the God of Jacob is our refuge.
Come, behold the works of the LORD,
    what desolations he has made in the earth.
He makes wars to cease unto the end of the earth;
    he breaks the bow, and cuts the spear in sunder;
    he burns the chariot in the fire.
Be still, and know that I am God:
I will be exalted among the nations,
    I will be exalted in the earth.

PSALM 46:1–3, 7–10, KJV, ADAPTED

PRAY

When the house doth sigh and weep,
And the world is drowned in sleep,
Yet my eyes the watch do keep,
Sweet Spirit comfort me!

ROBERT HERRICK, SEVENTEENTH CENTURY

REMEMBER Let there be a time today—if only for a moment—
when you tell yourself to be still and remember that God is God.

TRUST IN THE GRITTY DETAILS

Difficulty can challenge the most optimistic among us. Meeting difficulty requires more than resolve; if we are to keep going, we need the trust that is founded in the strength and staying power of God.

PRAY

Father, this day may bring some hard task to my life,
*   or some hard test of my love.*
I may grow tired, or despondent, or hopeless
*   in the midst or my routine.*
But Father, my whole life to this point has been
*   one great proof of your care.*
Bread has come for my body,
*   ideas to my mind,*
*   love to my heart,*
*   all from you.*
So help me, I beg of you,
*   while I stand on this side of all that the day may bring,*
to decide to trust you this day
*   to shine into any shadows of the mind,*
*   to stand by me in any trial of my love,*
*   and to give me rest in your good time, as I need it.*
May I so trust you today
*   that when the day is done my trust will be stronger than ever.*
Then, when my last day comes and my work is done,
*   may I trust you in death forever.*
In the Spirit of Jesus Christ our Lord, Amen.[15]
ROBERT COLLYER, NINETEENTH/TWENTIETH CENTURY, ADAPTED

REMEMBER If we let it, difficulty can deepen our trust and prove to us again that God will accompany us through everything.

MORE THAN KNOWLEDGE

Knowledge is highly valued in our culture. We are an information society. But knowledge is not the same as wisdom. Accumulating facts does not tell us how to live prudently or compassionately. Wisdom requires knowing not only *what* but also *who*—and *whose*—we are. God has much to show and teach us in this area. No wonder the proverb writer tells us that the beginning of wisdom is the fear of the Lord.

PRAY

Lord, give me a wise heart and discerning soul. May I grow today not only in the information I need for my job but also in the ways of the Spirit. I want to know more, but more than that I want to know you. Amen.

REMEMBER "For the LORD is good; his mercy is everlasting; and his truth endures to all generations" (Psalm 100:5, KJV, adapted).

TO THE HOLY SPIRIT

The grass withers, the flower fades,
  when the breath of the LORD blows upon it;
  surely the people are grass. . . .
But the word of our God will stand forever.
ISAIAH 40:7–8

PRAY

As the wind is your symbol
  so forward our goings.
As the dove
  so launch us heavenwards.
As water
  so purify our spirits.
As a cloud
  so cool our temptations.
As dew
  so revive our fatigue.
As fire
  so purge out our dross.
CHRISTINA ROSSETTI, NINETEENTH CENTURY

REMEMBER "God's goodness hath been great to thee; / Let never a day nor night unhallowed pass, / But still remember what the Lord hath done" (William Shakespeare, sixteenth/seventeenth century).

SUMMER

WHEN PRAYER BECOMES A TEST

Many times prayer just happens. Our heart overflows, or we are naturally driven to God for comfort. But other times only gritty will and sheer determination keep us at it. Might it be that in these times our faith shows its litmus colors?

PRAY

Today, Lord, I come out of faith as well as need. May my love for you weather the dry, shriveling times. Allow me to wait for the moist, loamy interludes. Help me pray whether I feel like it or not. Amen.

REMEMBER "Never give up prayer, and should you find dryness and difficulty, persevere in it for this very reason. God often desires to see what love your soul has, and love is not tried by ease and satisfaction" (St. John of the Cross, sixteenth century).[16]

OUR GREATEST THIRST

Sometimes we find ourselves surprised at our desertlike thirst for God. We secretly assume that the spiritual life should continue unbroken with rich and well-watered experiences of intimacy. But thirst may be the very thing that keeps us seeking. It reminds us how desolate and arid life would be without God's replenishing presence.

PRAY

O God, you are my God, I seek you,
my soul thirsts for you;
my flesh faints for you,
as in a dry and weary land where there is no water.
So I have looked upon you in the sanctuary,
beholding your power and glory.
Because your steadfast love is better than life,
my lips will praise you.

PSALM 63:1–3

REMEMBER Our thirst both draws and drives us to the God who alone can satisfy our longing.

THE CALLING

Sometimes, through circumstances or inattention, we more or less drift into our life's work. We count on a paycheck and hope for mildly interesting tasks, but we give little thought to how God can best use our aptitudes. Making it till the weekend's pursuits or dreaming about our next vacation pretty well exhausts our planning for the future. Are there ways in which you may be neglecting to take the long view and ask larger questions about where your work is taking you?

Take a moment to pray about your work. Tell God what you enjoy, and ask him how you can continue to serve him faithfully—day in and day out.

PRAY

Lord, let me know clearly
the work which you are calling me to do in life.
And grant me every grace I need to answer your call
with courage and love
and lasting dedication to your will. Amen.[17]

REMEMBER The word *vocation* has meaning for people other than those called to ministry or social work; this term recognizes that all work can have significance beyond the immediate task. Throughout the day, ask God to show you how your work can unfold as a calling, not just a job.

BROTHER SUN AND SISTER MOON

All around us, the world points to a creative genius, so much so that we can, through creation, see and hear and feel our way into God's goodness.

PRAY

Praise to you, my Lord, for all your creatures,
   especially for our brother sun,
   who makes the day and brings us light.
Through him you light the world with radiance
   and he reflects you and your splendor.
Praise to you, Lord, for our sister the moon, and the stars,
   which you have set clear and lovely in the sky.
Praise to you, Lord, for our brother the wind
   and for the air and clouds,
   for calm breezes and all weather
   by which you uphold life in all creatures.
Praise to you, my Lord, for sister water,
   who is useful and humble and precious and clean.
Praise to you, my Lord, for brother fire,
   by whom you light the night's darkness,
   for he is beautiful and playful and robust and strong.
Praise to you, my Lord, for our sister earth,
   who sustains and governs us
   and produces varied fruits and colored flowers and herbs....

ST. FRANCIS OF ASSISI, TWELFTH CENTURY, AUTHOR'S TRANSLATION

REMEMBER "The earth is the LORD's and all that is in it, the world, and those who live in it" (Psalm 24:1).

THE ULTIMATE IN CREATIVITY

In the beginning when God created the heavens and the earth, the earth was a formless void and darkness covered the face of the deep, while a wind from God swept over the face of the waters.

GENESIS 1:1–2

PRAY

Lord, sometimes my inner wells of creativity seem dry.
I need to bring things into being and produce,
> *but it is all I can do to go through the motions.*
I seem to have so little to offer.
Remind me that you authored creativity.
Even in the monotony of my task
> *you can show up to create in me*
> *something new, different, better.*
Amen.

REMEMBER The One who took a formless void and brought forth immense beauty and glory is creative beyond our imaginations. That God is still at work in the universe, in our little world, and even in our daily routines.

THE HEALING POWER OF REST

It is precisely when we are flooded with appointments and tasks and demands that we should remember our need for replenishment and rest. Work has a way of consuming all our time and focus. "Remember the sabbath day," the Bible urges us, "to keep it holy. Six days shalt thou labour, and do all thy work: But the seventh day is the sabbath of the LORD thy God: in it thou shalt not do any work" (Exodus 20:8–10, KJV).

In what ways can you pray today about restoring a healthy rhythm to your schedule?

PRAY

Lord, help me recover the balance of Sabbath in my frantic life. I don't want it as a hard legalism, but as a renewing discipline. May my times of rest not only refresh me personally but also renew me in your service. Amen.

REMEMBER Our work needs boundaries; otherwise it consumes, overwhelms, and depletes us. Only the holy "waste" of Sabbath (prayer, rest, and worship) gives us the energy and calm that allow us to work at our best.

REST THAT REJUVENATES

What we commonly call rest and relaxation (R and R) doesn't always refresh us deeply. A vacation at the shore or the museums may revive our sagging spirits, but our *souls* need Sabbaths. We need the renewing power of communion with God, the recuperative power of regular times of worship. Next time you attend church or pray, think of it not just as a duty but as a holiday for your soul.

PRAY

Lord, help me to find rest that goes deep.
In all my work, may I not become so frazzled or frantic
    that I lose sight of you
        and your power to refresh and make new.
Amen.

REMEMBER "So then, a sabbath rest still remains for the people of God; for those who enter God's rest also cease from their labors as God did from his. Let us therefore make every effort to enter that rest" (Hebrews 4:9–11).

TOUCHED BY ANGELS

We live in a world full of the unfathomable. Unseen heavenly forces accomplish their work with our barely noticing. Religious traditions the world over tell us that angels are part of the world God has made. Martin Luther wrote, "Although angels stand before the face and in the presence of God and his son Christ, yet they are hard by and about us."

PRAY

Everlasting God, you have ordained and constituted in a wonderful order the ministries of angels and mortals: Mercifully grant that, as your holy angels always serve and worship you in heaven, so by your appointment they may help and defend us here on earth; through Jesus Christ our Lord, who lives and reigns with you and the Holy Spirit, one God, for ever and ever. Amen.

THE BOOK OF COMMON PRAYER

REMEMBER More than you may realize, the world of the celestial and eternal intersects our daily life. This can give you cause for hope—and reverence.

THE DELIGHT THAT BECOMES GOD

We may not have ears for it, but creation testifies continually to God's goodness. "The mountains and the hills before you," promised the prophet Isaiah, "shall burst into song, and all the trees of the field shall clap their hands" (Isaiah 55:12). Here is another poet's rousing picture of praise:

Sing, my soul, to God who made you,
Raise to heaven your grateful voice;
All God's creatures, singing, call you:
In his goodness now rejoice.
Pure and holy love unbounded
Fills God's heart tender and kind;
All who truly serve him find
Rest, by God's strong arm surrounded.
PAUL GERHARDT, SEVENTEENTH CENTURY, ADAPTED; TRANSLATED
FROM GERMAN TO ENGLISH BY O. E. WIELAND, NINETEENTH CENTURY

PRAY

Lord, make me mindful so that I don't miss expressing the delight that becomes you. Give me a heart to praise and sing, even if I do so only in the quiet of my heart and my little spot at work. Amen.

REMEMBER Our world is so full of goodness that worship and praise come naturally. But the impulse can be buried and the songs drowned out.

TO STAY MOVING

The life of faith is not so much standing still as moving forward. Not sitting in perpetual rest, but pressing on. Spiritual writers have for centuries spoken of growth as a journey. We follow the Spirit's leading into areas that may seem strange or new, like Abraham, who "set out, not knowing where he was going" (Hebrews 11:8).

Is God drawing you into some new territory of faithfulness or service? Ask God now.

PRAY

Lord, help me continue to want to stay on the journey. I want to sojourn like Abraham, to keep moving into that exciting future you hold out ahead. And remind me that just as you have shown me countless roads and paths in the past, you can be trusted to reward my longings with new adventures ahead. Amen.

REMEMBER We do more than hold on to the certainties of faith; we also allow God to point us in new directions.

GOD IN WHO I AM AND WHAT I DO

Sometimes we picture God as aloof and far out of reach. But the truest spiritual traditions remind us that however majestic and high God may be, he is also near.

PRAY

God be in my head,
and in my understanding.
God be in my eyes,
and in my looking.
God be in my mouth,
and in my speaking.
God be in my heart,
and in my thinking.
God be at my end,
and at my departing.

SARUM PRIMER, SIXTEENTH CENTURY

REMEMBER "Draw nigh to God, and he will draw nigh to you" (James 4:8, KJV).

THE BREAD THAT SATISFIES

It is not hard to think of our spiritual stirrings as a hunger. Jesus must have had this metaphor in mind when he said, "Blessed are those who hunger and thirst for righteousness, for they will be filled" (Matthew 5:6). Fortunately we can feed on more than spiritual junk food, high in calories but low in substance. We can fill our souls with the satisfying Bread of Life.

PRAY

Lord, forgive me for munching on pale substitutes, for wanting microwave convenience. I want my hunger to lead me to you, who alone can satisfy my hunger. May I this day be mindful, in my many tasks and duties, of your sustaining presence. Let me feed on you and every day find true life in your goodness. Amen.

REMEMBER "The actions of our Savior are so rich in meaning that every soul that ponders them finds in them its own share of spiritual food to nourish it and bring it to salvation" (St. Catherine of Siena, fourteenth century).

THE HEART-HUNGER

We sometimes feel powerless to do much about the state of the world. But kindnesses—our small gestures and little acts—carry impressive power. Through kindness we can make a difference in our everyday world.

PRAY

Lord, help me to show toward [others] that kindness which I have so often craved from them. May I think of my neighbor not as my rival who would undo me, but as my brother [or sister] who needs me. Give me the compassion of Jesus that I may never be able to turn coldly from anyone who needs me. Make me quick to hear the cry of the suffering. Turn my feet toward the house of sorrow. May I know the joy of carrying hope to hearts that have long been strangers to hope.... Help me to relieve the heart-hunger of the neglected. For Jesus' sake. Amen.[18]

REMEMBER "I expect to pass through this life but once. If therefore, there be any kindness that I can show, or any good thing I can do to any fellow being, let me do it now, and not defer or neglect it, as I shall not pass this way again" (Stephen Grellet, eighteenth/nineteenth century).

WHEN ANOTHER SPEAKS HARSHLY

Keep what is worth keeping—
And with a breath of kindness
Blow the rest away.[19]
DINAH MARIA MULOCK CRAIK, NINETEENTH CENTURY

PRAY

Lord, too often I lash out when someone says a harsh word. I react defensively or shoot back blame and criticism, or at least I do in the privacy of my fantasizing heart. Keep my relationships pure and clean, O Lord. Please grant me a supernatural large-ness of heart and openness of mind. Allow me to overcome cutting words with your life-giving love. In the name of Jesus, who chose to love even his ill-wishers and persecutors. Amen.

REMEMBER "You must understand this, my beloved: let everyone be quick to listen, slow to speak, slow to anger" (James 1:19).

THE PROBLEMS WE CANNOT AVOID

We would prefer to believe that we can escape suffering, that somehow we will end up exempt from heartache. But life frequently confronts us with difficulties we cannot explain and problems we cannot avoid. We don't need to be thrown out of balance by this, not if we remember that God sees us and draws close to us—even in the hard and harsh moments.

PRAY

I say to God my Rock,
*   "Why have you forgotten me?*
Why must I go about mourning,
*   oppressed by the enemy?"*
My bones suffer mortal agony
*   as my foes taunt me,*
saying to me all day long,
*   "Where is your God?"*
Why are you downcast, O my soul?
*   Why so disturbed within me?*
Put your hope in God,
*   for I will yet praise him,*
*   my Savior and my God.*

PSALM 42:9–11, NIV

REMEMBER No matter the situation, you can say with the psalmist, "I will yet praise God."

WHO MAKES US WHOLE

We can't literally look at Jesus. But we can turn our inner eyes toward him, using our imagination to see the goodness he embodies and to perceive his presence, which pervades our days.

PRAY

Jesus, I am resting, resting,
in the joy of what you are;
I am finding out the greatness
of your loving heart.
You have bid me gaze upon you,
and your beauty fills my soul,
For by your transforming power,
you have made me whole.

Ever lift your face upon me
that in waiting I may see
Resting 'neath your smile, Lord Jesus,
earth's dark shadows flee.
Brightness of my Father's glory,
sunshine of my Father's face,
Keep me ever trusting, resting,
fill me with your grace.

JEAN SOPHIA PIGOTT, NINETEENTH CENTURY, ADAPTED

REMEMBER We all need a smiling face at times. How kind of God to grace our world with the face of Jesus—in his earthly life and now, through Christ's ongoing presence.

THE PERFORMANCE TRAP

Our jobs can condition us to measure ourselves against last year's results. Or we gauge a product's impact against last year's profits. We may transfer such bottom-line thinking to our habits of prayer. Pause now and turn to God, bringing with you any feelings of not measuring up, asking for God's mercy and grace so that you can feel forgiven and free.

PRAY

Just as I am, without one plea,
But that Thy blood was shed for me,
And that Thou bidst me come to Thee,
O Lamb of God, I come, I come.

Just as I am, Thou wilt receive,
Wilt welcome, pardon, cleanse, relieve;
Because Thy promise I believe,
O Lamb of God, I come, I come.
CHARLOTTE ELLIOTT, NINETEENTH CENTURY

Lord, I call upon you and the mercy you have provided through
your Son, Jesus. Imperfect I certainly am. Thank you that my
imperfection doesn't mean that I can't come to you. In the life-
giving name of Jesus. Amen.

REMEMBER How good to know that we don't need to wait until we can come as we should be but that we can come as we are.

WHAT CAN GO WRONG

Our minds are ingenious at thinking up things that could go wrong. Sometimes we are plagued by an eternal conversation filled with the worst outcomes. What if I don't do well on the job? What if my child rejects me? What if I fail to live a good life? In one sense such fears are natural.

In another sense they can rob us of joy and true freedom. "A day of worry is more exhausting than a day of work," one nineteenth-century observer noted. When we work *and* worry, we can really wear ourselves down.

Perhaps more than any other practice, prayer gives us a place to turn and find our worries transformed. Turn your times of anxiety into occasions to turn to the Lord for help.

PRAY
How I need your help, O Lord! Let me not distrust you but hear your clear promises to care for me through every circumstance, even the worst I can imagine.

REMEMBER "Only one kind of worry is correct: to worry that you worry too much" (Jewish proverb).

LABOR'S TRUEST REWARD

Whatever your task, put yourselves into it, as done for the Lord and not for your masters, since you know that from the Lord you will receive the inheritance as your reward; you serve the Lord Christ.

COLOSSIANS 3:23–24

PRAY

Dear Lord, teach me to be generous.
Teach me to serve you as you deserve,
To give and not to count the cost,
To fight and not to heed the wounds,
To toil and not to seek for rest,
To labor and not see reward,
Except that of knowing that I do
your will.[20]

ST. IGNATIUS OF LOYOLA, SIXTEENTH CENTURY

REMEMBER Some of work's greatest satisfactions come not from the measurable result or bottom line but from the knowledge that we have done what we can and should.

TAKING CARE OF BUSYNESS

Most of us don't lack for things to do. But we may lack the sense of knowing *why* we do what we do. Activism as a habit or condition of the heart won't sustain our work. Only a larger sense of the whole keeps us going. Ultimately, only God's presence can renew us and refresh us for all he calls us to do and be.

PRAY

Lord, you have been our dwelling place
  throughout all generations.
Before the mountains were born
  or you brought forth the earth and the world,
  from everlasting to everlasting you are God....
Teach us to number our days aright,
  that we may gain a heart of wisdom....
Satisfy us in the morning with your unfailing love,
  that we may sing for joy and be glad all our days.

PSALM 90:1–2, 12, 14, NIV

REMEMBER Activity without purpose leaves us frustrated, deflated, even despairing.

WHERE TO FIND JOY

The impression we often get from the culture around us is that happiness comes to those who grab for it. "Take care of yourself" becomes a kind of watchword. Feeling good is a mandate. But sages through the centuries continually underscored the hollowness of such thinking. Happiness is not a goal but a byproduct. Make it your aim, and it eludes you. Joy comes when we lose our self-absorption in concern for others. It comes from opening ourselves to let God fill us with goodness. You cannot grasp it; you can only receive it.

PRAY

Lord, I am tempted to think that living for you or caring deeply about others leads to drudgery. But then you remind me that it is precisely the opposite. Help me think about you more. Let me stay as alert to the needs and hopes of those around me as I am to my own needs. Don't let my focus on my own needs blind me to the joy and wonder of a life lived outside itself.

REMEMBER In giving yourself away and holding lightly to what you own, you experience more freedom, deeper joy, greater peace.

CAN YOU EARN IT? HARDLY

Something in us very much likes the accomplished feeling of knowing we worked hard. We're uncomfortable with simply being given something. Yet in many areas of life, prayer certainly one of them, we must rely on grace—God's unearned favor. "But God, being rich in faithful love, through the great love with which he loved us, even when we were dead in our sins, brought us to life with Christ—it is through grace that you have been saved—and raised us up with him and gave us a place with him in heaven, in Christ Jesus" (Ephesians 2:4–6, NJB).

PRAY

Lord, today help me rely on you. I have many plans and projects. Sometimes I get so caught up in them that I forget how much rests on you and your purposes. I overestimate my ability to make things happen. I forget the place of grace. Help me do better in that regard, even if it takes some doing on your part.

REMEMBER Our standing with God is a matter not of impressing or earning but of receiving.

AMAZING!

Amazing grace! How sweet the sound
that saved a wretch like me!
I once was lost but now am found,
was blind but now I see.

The Lord has promised good to me,
his word my hope secures;
he will my shield and portion be
as long as life endures.

Through many dangers, toils and snares,
I have already come;
'tis grace that brought me safe thus far,
and grace will lead me home.

JOHN NEWTON, EIGHTEENTH CENTURY

PRAY

*Lord, how great is your love! How wonderful is your goodness
toward me! Forgive me when in my mental fogginess or my
soul's forgetfulness I take for granted all that you have done, all
that you offer, all that you promise. Amen.*

REMEMBER The Lord has promised wonderful things to us.
Amazing!

HONEST TO GOD

We often fear telling God what is honestly on our minds, and our reticence leaves us feeling distant. We don't come at all, waiting for the day when we have our emotions "together." But why leave God out of the equation? We need to pray most when we're at our neediest and most irritable.

PRAY

Bow down your ear, O LORD, hear me:
   for I am poor and needy.
Preserve my soul....
O you who are my God,
save your servant who trusts in you.

PSALM 86:1–2, KJV, ADAPTED

REMEMBER God would prefer you to come honestly than not at all.

GOD IN THE DETAILS

So much of life happens in our daily arenas—factory, office, shopping mall, school, home. God is present in these little moments, too: when we kiss a loved one good-bye in the morning, browse through magazines while we wait for a doctor's appointment, stand at a sink doing dishes. God works in moments, says a French proverb.

PRAY

God, remind me that you are present in the flat stretches of life and daily detours, not just the milestones and big twists. Help me have eyes today to see traces of your work, places of your moving. In Jesus' name. Amen.

REMEMBER God sometimes seems to hide his work, as François Fénelon wrote, under an unnoticeable sequence of events.

A SPACIOUS PLACE

A friend once likened a difficult time of life to getting stuck in a "deep, narrow, muddy pit." There were days, she said, she just chose to sit in the mud. Most people can recall closed-in periods of discouragement. Options seem blocked. It is hard to see much beyond those confining walls. A job may feel that way after a while.

Perhaps it is no accident that one of the Old Testament words for salvation translates as "to make wide or spacious."

PRAY

[You] have not delivered me into the hand of the enemy;
you have set my feet in a broad place.
Be gracious to me, O LORD, for I am in distress;
my eye wastes away from grief,
my soul and body also....
But I trust in you, O LORD;
I say, "You are my God."
My times are in your hand;
deliver me from the hand of my enemies and persecutors.
Let your face shine upon your servant;
save me in your steadfast love.

PSALM 31:8–9, 14–16

REMEMBER Over and over, God puts us in a place where we can stretch and grow.

WHEN WORK WEARIES US

We hear that some of you are living in idleness, mere busybodies, not doing any work. Now such persons we command and exhort in the Lord Jesus Christ to do their work quietly and to earn their own living. Brothers and sisters, do not be weary in doing what is right.

2 THESSALONIANS 3:11–13

PRAY

O God, who has commanded that no one should be idle, give us grace to employ all our talents and faculties in the service appointed for us; that, whatever our hand finds to do, we may do it with energy. Help us go cheerfully on in the road that you have marked out, not wanting too earnestly that it should be either smoother or wider; but, daily seeking our way by your light, may we trust ourselves and the end of our journey to you, the fountain of joy, and sing songs of praise as we go along. Then, O Lord, receive us at the gate of life that you have opened for us in Christ Jesus. Amen.

MARTINEAU'S COMMON PRAYER FOR CHRISTIAN WORSHIP, ADAPTED

REMEMBER When we submit to God, God comes alongside us to help. No matter how weary we feel, just the thought of God can renew us and keep us from giving up.

A LOOK AROUND—AND UP

It's so easy to lose sight of realities outside our immediate range. But sometimes a look around reminds us of realities above us, realities that infiltrate daily life and invade our routine with a gracious presence.

PRAY

O LORD, our Sovereign,

   how majestic is your name in all the earth! . . .
When I look at your heavens, the work of your fingers,
   the moon and the stars that you have established;
what are human beings that you are mindful of them,
   mortals that you care for them?

PSALM 8:1, 3–4

REMEMBER God is all around. Sometimes all we must do is slow down enough to be able to notice and see God's splendor. A mere look out the window can become an exercise in spiritual recollection!

A HUMBLE HEART

Technology creates the illusion that we control life. My computer allows me to write paragraphs that I can then endlessly revise with a couple of keystrokes. In an instant I can send an E-mail message to my friend in New Zealand or my brother in China.

At the same time, so much lies outside my control. So much has to do with letting myself be carried along, not in passivity, but in acceptance.

Spiritual writer Jean Pierre de Caussade once wrote that the soul yielded to God can allow itself to be gently carried like a feather on a breeze, responding to every movement of God's grace like a balloon aloft in the air.

PRAY

Lord, I try so hard to grasp things and guarantee certain outcomes. Give me a more accepting approach to my colleagues, my friends, my family—any person and every situation. Remind me that they are not commodities to trade in, projects to fix, or accessories to make me look good. Help me give people room to grow and flourish. And help me remember that I don't control the world but that you are king of the universe. All things find meaning and direction in you.

REMEMBER Try to picture yourself with the lightness of a balloon and with carefree sensitivity to the currents of God's Spirit that blow through your life.

BETTER TO PRAY THAN FRET

Do you ever worry that your prayers are trivial to God? It's good to remember that the portrait of God we get in the Bible encourages us: "Do not be anxious about anything," the apostle Paul said, "but in everything, by prayer and petition, with thanksgiving, present your requests to God" (Philippians 4:6, NIV). It is as though God were reassuring us that if it is important enough to worry about, perhaps it is important enough to pray about.

PRAY

Lord, you invite me to come asking, unafraid that what I ask may be too small. So now I pray, asking for your aid in these troubling matters (think of your own list).

Listen to my cry for help,
my King and my God,
for to you I pray.
PSALM 5:2, NIV

REMEMBER "Anxious for nothing, prayerful for everything, thankful for anything" (D. L. Moody, nineteenth century).

HOLY BROKENNESS

We like to think of ourselves as "together" people. We work hard to present our best face to others. But there is a place for a kind of holy brokenness. When we stop trying so hard—with God, with those we relate to at home, with our coworkers—we leave room for God to move in and fill us with sustaining strength. In the long run, we will find ourselves going farther and lasting longer than if we pretended to be self-sufficient.

PRAY

We ask you, O Lord, with whom is the fountain of life, and without whom we can do nothing, whose grace is enough for us, and whose strength is made perfect in weakness, to live in us, that we, keeping your commandments, may reside in your love. So will our peace be like a flowing river, and our righteousness like the strong waves of the sea. Through Jesus Christ our Lord. Amen.

JOHN H. B. MONSELL, NINETEENTH CENTURY, ADAPTED

REMEMBER "Hope in God; for I shall again praise him, my help and my God" (Psalm 43:5).

HEALTHY FEAR AND TREMBLING

We don't seek God because we were brilliant enough to think of it. God started the process long before we were even born. Our relationship with God is first of all a gift, and when we receive him, God shows us he is already at work in us. We have a role in all of this, of course. Our part is to make room for God and God's ways. And we work out what God is already doing in us in practical settings: on the job, at our home, in the neighborhood.

PRAY

O Lord, who sees that all hearts are empty unless you fill them, all desires thwarted unless they long for you; give us grace to seek and find you, that we may be yours and you may be ours forever. Amen.

CHRISTINA ROSSETTI, NINETEENTH CENTURY, ADAPTED

REMEMBER "Work out your own salvation with fear and trembling; for it is God who is at work in you, enabling you both to will and to work for his good pleasure" (Philippians 2:12–13).

AN INSTRUMENT OF PEACE

No one naturally relishes working in a climate of conflict and injured feelings. But perhaps God has placed you where you are to sow seeds of another spirit and a gentler approach. Pray that God will use you to nurture peace wherever you find yourself today.

PRAY

Lord, make me an instrument of your peace.

Where there is hatred, let me sow love,

Where there is injury, pardon,

Where there is doubt, faith,

Where there is despair, hope,

Where there is darkness, light,

Where there is sadness, joy.

O Divine Master, grant that I may not so much seek to be consoled as to console,

not so much to be understood as to understand,

not so much to be loved as to love;

for it is in giving that we receive,

it is in pardoning that we are pardoned,

it is in dying that we awake to eternal life.[21]

AUTHOR UNKNOWN

REMEMBER "Blessed are the peacemakers, for they will be called children of God" (Matthew 5:9).

NOT VERY FLASHY, BUT VERY REAL

The world in general has its own definition of a satisfying life, but "the good life," for all its seductive appeal, often only appears to be fulfilling. On the other hand, the Christian life comes up wanting when it comes to dazzle, convenience, and flashiness. But concerning the deepest and more lasting satisfaction, nothing compares to the life of faith.

PRAY

O Lord, my God, you represent to me everything that is good.
Remember me because I am little and have nothing.
You alone are good and I can do nothing without you.
You can do all things, accomplish all things, fill all things.
Remember your mercies
and fill my heart with your grace,
you that will that no work be done in vain.
Do not turn your face away from me or
withdraw your comforting presence,
lest my soul become as a thirsty land to you.
Teach me, I pray, to do your will
and live humbly and worthily in your sight.
Amen.

THOMAS À KEMPIS, FOURTEENTH/FIFTEENTH CENTURY

REMEMBER The satisfactions of living a life pleasing to God last and last.

THE LIMITS OF LIP SERVICE ALONE

"Hypocrites!" This epithet has been flung many times at those who concern themselves with God. It is true of all of us, perhaps, that our lives do not often enough match what we profess to believe. When we discover this about ourselves, it should drive us not to despair but to prayer.

PRAY

O Lord,

the Lord whose ways are right,

keep us from lip service and empty forms.

From having a name that we live,

but being dead.

Help us to worship you

by righteous deeds and lives of holiness.

CHRISTINA ROSSETTI, NINETEENTH CENTURY

REMEMBER Throughout the day, remember today's prayer. Continue to ask God to help you become what you should be and, through God's help, what you can be.

COME!

When nightfall or gloomy shadows come, we can do more than complain about the darkness. We can wait for the coming of light. We can pray for the Light of the World to offer his radiance.

PRAY

Come, true light.

Come, everlasting life.

Come, unseen mystery.

Come, treasure without category.

Come, rejoicing without end.

Come, light that knows no nightfall.

Come, raising of the fallen.

Come, resurrection of the dead.

Come, for you are yourself the desire deep within me.

Come, my breath and my life.

Come, the encouragement for my humble soul.

Come, my happiness, my glory, my everliving delight.[22]

ST. SYMEON THE NEW THEOLOGIAN, TENTH/ELEVENTH CENTURY, ADAPTED

REMEMBER "Our Lord, come!" (1 Corinthians 16:22).

WHY WE ARE RESTLESS

When we are quiet enough to notice, we discover that deep within us is a great longing. We often define this restless yearning with the vocabulary of our daily circumstances: If only I had a better job, a more sensitive family, a larger income, or more time, *then* life would be fine. But when we attend to our restlessness, we discover that ultimately it has spiritual roots. Becoming aware of that longing always brings an implicit invitation to pray.

PRAY

O God, in whom and by whom all things live,
you command us to seek you,

and are ready to be found.

You invite us to knock

and you open when we do.

To know you

is life.

To serve you

is freedom.

To praise you

is the soul's joy and delight.

Guard me with the power of your grace

here and in all places.

Now

and at all times, forever. Amen.

ST. AUGUSTINE, FOURTH/FIFTH CENTURY, ADAPTED

REMEMBER We forget sometimes, but the deepest restlessness within us comes from our soul's longing for God.

TO TELL THE TRUTH

It is not always easy to tell the truth. We usually fudge or tell lies out of fear of criticism. So truth takes courage. It may incur a boss's wrath. It may make us look foolish. Being a truthful person takes a willingness to brave another's displeasure or ridicule. So how do we become truthful? Ask God for courage today, courage not to shrink from the truths God has given you to tell.

PRAY

Lord, in whom is the truth, help us, we ask, to speak the truth in love, to hate telling lies, to refuse to speak with exaggeration, shading, or airs. And if trouble or even persecution comes for the sake of the truth, let us not be put off.

CHRISTINA ROSSETTI, NINETEENTH CENTURY, ADAPTED

REMEMBER "When you add to the truth, you subtract from it" (Talmud).

MUSIC IN THE AIR

Just above my head,
I hear music in the air;
There must be a God somewhere.[23]
AFRICAN AMERICAN SPIRITUAL

Sometimes cocking your ear can make all the difference. You can hear a dull grind or a kind of music, depending on how you listen. Why not approach the sounds of your day—hallway conversations, machinery noises, everyday traffic rhythms—as part of a symphony of life? And then why not join in the music with your own sounds and words (and maybe even a quiet song)?

PRAY

Lord, I want to join creation's symphony of praise. Let me not mumble or grumble but declare and even sing the wonders of your goodness. Amen.

REMEMBER O give thanks to the LORD; call upon his name: make known his deeds among the people. Sing to him, sing psalms unto him: talk of all his wondrous works" (Psalm 105:1–2, KJV, adapted).

HELP!

There are times when the most direct and unvarnished prayers make the most sense. When a crisis leaves us up to our noses in stress or panic, we can ask for God's saving, comforting help. Our inner cry for help can become a cry to God: "Help!"

Such a prayer embraces any feeling we experience, and it fits any situation or challenge.

PRAY

Do not withhold your tender mercies from me, O LORD:
*   let your lovingkindness and your truth*
*   continually preserve me.*
For troubles beyond counting surround me
*   and my own wrongdoing has taken hold of me*
*   so that I am not able to look up....*
Be pleased, O LORD, to deliver me: O LORD, make haste to help me.

PSALM 40:11–13, KJV, ADAPTED

REMEMBER "[For cultivating awareness of God, keep in mind this verse]: 'O God, make speed to save me: O Lord, make haste to help me.' . . . It contains an invocation of God against every danger, a humble confession of faith, a note of reverent regard, an acknowledgment of our weakness, a confidence in the answer, and the assurance of ever-present help. For one who is constantly calling on his protector is certain that he is always at hand" (St. John Cassian, fourth/fifth century, adapted).

IF WE CANNOT LOVE OUR WORK

You may not think of your satisfaction level on the job as a spiritual issue, but it is. We work too many hours for God to waste the time we spend on the job. Whatever you do, how you feel about your work certainly should be a matter for praying and listening.

PRAY

Almighty God, we bless and praise you
> *that we have wakened to the light of another day.*
Now we will think of what a day should be.
Our days are yours,
> *let them be spent for you.*
Our days are relatively few,
> *let them be spent with care.*
There are dark days behind us,
> *forgive us their sinfulness.*
There may be dark days ahead of us,
> *strengthen us for their challenges.*
We pray that you would shine on this day,
> *the day we may call our own.*
Help us to take pleasure in our daily work.
Show us clearly what our duty is and
> *help us to be faithful in it.*
Let all we do be well done, fit for your eye to see.
Give us strength to do, patience to bear, courage never to quit.
When we cannot love our work
> *help us think of it as your task.*
By our true love for you,
> *make unlovely things shine*
> *in the light of your great love.*
Amen.

GEORGE DAWSON, NINETEENTH CENTURY, ADAPTED

REMEMBER "Always give yourselves fully to the work of the Lord, because you know that your labor in the Lord is not in vain" (1 Corinthians 15:58, NIV).

MORE THAN GOOD INTENTIONS

Sometimes what we intend and what we actually do differ dramatically. Living a faithful life, however, means trading pious fantasies for honest effort, idle wishes for actions. Are there ways God is calling you to act today?

PRAY

O Lord, we commit ourselves to your care and keeping this day.
Let your grace be mighty in us
    and sufficient in us,
    and let it work in us
        both to intend and to do what you want.
Grant us strength for the duties of the day.
Keep us from sin,
    give us mastery over our own spirits,
    and help us to avoid speaking rashly with our lips....
Prepare us for all the events of the day,
    for we cannot, of course, know what a day will bring.
Give us grace to deny our whims,
    to take up our cross daily,
    and to follow in the steps of our Lord and Master. Amen.
MATTHEW HENRY, SEVENTEENTH/EIGHTEENTH CENTURY, ADAPTED

REMEMBER "For we are what he has made us, created in Christ Jesus for good works, which God prepared beforehand to be our way of life" (Ephesians 2:10).

ARE YOU STABLE?

Monastic communities have for centuries advocated the value of what they call stability. The word suggests that a monk promises to *stay* in the monastery and not question whether or not he should go elsewhere. In a way, all of us can subscribe to the idea behind this ideal. We could enjoy great rewards for not always and everywhere thinking of the *next* neighborhood, the *next* relationship, the *next* job, or the *next* career move.

PRAY

Whether I fly with angels, fall with dust,
Your hands made both, and I am there:
Your power and love, my love and trust
Make one place everywhere.

GEORGE HERBERT, SEVENTEENTH CENTURY

REMEMBER We need to learn to be present where we are, giving ourselves fully to the work or opportunity as it is, trusting God to move us along if required.

A PATTERN FOR LIFE

We generally spend a fair amount of time on our appearance. We worry about what we look like, how we will come across to others. It is no surprise that the Bible pays attention to our "image" from a different angle. It speaks of being conformed not to what is most fashionable but to what is most lasting. Not to what is popular but to what is faithful. Wise teachers tell us that the likeness we are to strive for most is that of God.

PRAY

My God, I wholeheartedly thank you
*   for all your goodness to my body and my soul.*
I want your guidance and direction
*   in all I do.*
Let your wisdom counsel me,
*   your hand lead me,*
*   and your arm support me.*
I put myself into your hands.
Breathe into my soul holy and heavenly desires.
Conform me to your own likeness.
Make me like my Savior.
Enable me in some measure to live here on earth as he lived,
and to act in all things as he would have acted. Amen.
ASHTON ORENDON, NINETEENTH CENTURY, ADAPTED

REMEMBER What could it mean for you today if Christ, not the latest celebrity, became your pattern?

COMPLETELY ALIVE

For some people, *religion* is never a word to use in the same breath with words like *lively* or *exhilarating*. A nineteenth-century poet captured such an assumption about Jesus: "Pale Galilean, the world has grown gray in your breath."

But that is not the picture we get in the Bible—where the word *life* appears over five hundred times. Jesus said he came that people would "have life, and have it to the full" (John 10:10, NIV). Are there ways in which you long for a richer life? Have you perhaps neglected turning to the author of life to search for it in and from him?

PRAY

Lord, you have created life, and you still breathe life into all living things. May my life reflect yours. Help me find in Jesus the way to you and to a more abundant life. Amen.

REMEMBER "The glory of God is a person completely alive" (St. Irenaeus, third century).

WHEN HOPE GETS SHAKEN

We all face situations that make it easy to lose a sense of possibility and hope. Often we need courage simply to keep going. A strong hope does not come from thin air but from a bedrock conviction about who God is. A lasting hope requires an everlasting God, the God whose portrait the Bible paints so graphically.

PRAY

Lord, enkindle in me a growing and unshakable hope.
I sometimes face situations that appear impossible.
I deal with relationships that leave me floundering.
I wade through tasks that seem well beyond me.

Remind me that you are not a small God,
*   but a God worthy of a large and lasting hope. Amen.*

REMEMBER "Let them give thanks to the Lord for his unfailing love and his wonderful deeds for men, for he breaks down gates of bronze and cuts through bars of iron" (Psalm 107:15–16, NIV).

HELP FOR DIFFICULT RELATIONSHIPS

God delights in healthy relationships. If you are having trouble relating to someone at work, be assured that God happily entertains prayers for reconciliation. Ask God now for help in any difficult relationship. And then listen for any marching orders that may come.

PRAY

O God, from whom proceeds all that is good and right, give me the promised peace that the world cannot give. When my heart is settled and made ready and able to obey your ways, help love flow freely toward all with whom I must relate. Give me grace to make peace. Amen.

REMEMBER "Bless your persecutors; never curse them, bless them. Rejoice with others when they rejoice, and be sad with those in sorrow. Give the same consideration to all others alike. . . . Never pay back evil with evil, but bear in mind the ideals that all regard with respect. As much as possible, and to the utmost of your ability, be at peace with everyone. Never try to get revenge" (Romans 12:14–19, NJB).

PRAYERS TO A KIND GOD

We all have times when our smarts and charm and self-confidence run dry. At those times we realize (in a way we don't when things go well) that we feel empty, directionless, even desolate. We need to turn to Someone whose love and patience never run out.

PRAY

Be kind to me,
merciful, sweet, and gracious Lord,
and grant to me,
your poor needy creature,
at least some of the time
to feel in a small way
your strong, affectionate love.
Grant this day that my faith may become stronger,
my hope in your goodness increased,
and my love, once kindled in me,
may never fail.

THOMAS À KEMPIS, FOURTEENTH/FIFTEENTH CENTURY, ADAPTED

REMEMBER "God soon turns from his wrath, but he never turns from his love" (Charles Spurgeon, nineteenth century).

A PRAYER FOR DISCERNMENT

For all our training and resources and information, we still get confused. We live in what someone has called fact fog and data smog. So many voices, so many perspectives, so many urgent and strident causes. Sometimes we need not so much to sort it all out by will or intellect as to discern through a heart made pliable and wise to the things of the Spirit.

Such wisdom comes through praying and meditating on the Lord's word and works.

PRAY

Lord, give me grace
to understand what is worth knowing,
to value what is most valuable to you,
to cherish what you cherish,
to abhor what displeases you or hurts another.
Amen.

REMEMBER "If any of you is lacking in wisdom, ask God, who gives to all generously and ungrudgingly, and it will be given you. But ask in faith, never doubting, for the one who doubts is like a wave of the sea, driven and tossed by the wind" (James 1:5–6).

THE BASIS OF BEING BETTER

We tend to rest calmly in God's favor when we think we have done well. We find it easier to turn to him when feeling good about ourselves. But doing so only gets things turned around. God's gracious, generous love is never something we earn, even on our best days.

PRAY

Lord, I get weary of always trying to make myself over, make myself presentable. Give me courage to come to you to seek the wonderful help you offer. You alone can help me become what I long to be and what you know I can be. In Jesus' name. Amen.

REMEMBER God's grace, said St. Augustine centuries ago, "is given not because we have done good works, but so that we may be able to do them."

OUR STAMMERING VOICE

Prayer has far more to do with earnestness than eloquence.
More to do with God's listening ear than our stammering
voice. It is the language not of rule books and score keeping
but of relationship and freely offered mercy.

PRAY

Lord, I sometimes forget that I come to you at your invitation,
*   not by my blustering self-promotion.*
I approach at all because you love me in all my waywardness
*   and long to lure me back.*
Help me stay both humble about who I am
*   and assured of your forgiving, receiving grace.*
When I come to my senses and see how much I need you,
*   may I always hear your gracious, beckoning call.*

REMEMBER In Jesus' story of the wayward son who stumbled
home (the parable of the prodigal son), the young man's father
ran to meet him and embrace him as soon as he could see him
coming. Is our heavenly Father any different?

THE PEOPLE WE LOVE TO HATE

No job setting comes without them: People who require extra patience. People who make us bite our tongues to keep from spitting out a caustic comeback. People we love to hate.

Who are these people in your life? Think for a moment about how you can convert the energy you spend fuming over them into an impulse to pray for them.

PRAY

Lord, help me deal with the annoying, cloying, nasty people I know. Give me gentleness toward them, even when I convince myself that they could never deserve it. In place of my diseased and faltering heart, please transplant Jesus' gutsy, constant compassion. In Jesus' name and through his strengthening power. Amen.

REMEMBER "Nothing makes us love a person so much as praying for him or her" (William Law, seventeenth/eighteenth century).

IS IT ENOUGH—EVER?

A wise person does not care for what he or she cannot have.
GEORGE HERBERT, SEVENTEENTH CENTURY

PRAY

Lord, help us by prayer
    to hold tightly to you
    and by love to cling to you,
        our constant help.
We ask you, when your providences are dark to our eyes,
    strengthen our faith.
Whatever portion you allot as ours,
    give us grace to say,
        It is enough. Amen.

CHRISTINA ROSSETTI, NINETEENTH CENTURY, ADAPTED

REMEMBER Contentment has less to do with what we think we will get and more to do with noticing the blessings we already have—not what we manage to accumulate, but what we learn to appreciate, small or large.

OUR AWKWARDNESS IN BELIEVING

Fools say in their hearts, "There is no God." . . .
The Lord looks down from heaven on humankind
    to see if there are any who are wise,
    who seek after God.

PSALM 14:1–2

PRAY

Lord, sometimes the things I believe about you make me stand out awkwardly from the crowd. Some people seem threatened by my spiritual enthusiasm or my concern about doing right. At times I think it would be easier not to believe in you at all. Help me stand and live out constancy toward you and compassion for others, even when the rewards are a fuzzy memory or a fading hope.

REMEMBER Wherever you are, whatever you face, God sees and knows and will not leave you stranded.

IT'S A BIG WORLD

At times we try to limit others or ourselves to narrow categories. Any experience outside of ours must be suspect. We end up passing judgment on those who do not fit into the patterns we can account for. But when we presume to know so much, we cease to grow. Life becomes more comfortable, yes, but we close ourselves off from discovery. We fold our arms and close our hands to gifts that come only from unexpected places and unlikely people.

PRAY

O Lord, help me not to despise or oppose what I do not understand.
WILLIAM PENN, SEVENTEENTH/EIGHTEENTH CENTURY

REMEMBER "Still round the corner there may wait, / A new road, or a secret gate" (J. R. R. Tolkien, twentieth century).[24]

YOUR HIDDEN VOCATION

Not every job comes with an obviously high sense of calling. Many jobs are filled with repetition or busywork that seems meaningless. And no job—no matter how fabulous or profound it appears—is constantly glorious or important. How do we keep the larger picture in view?

One way is to remind ourselves why we do what we do. Perhaps we do it for no reason other than to pay the rent or mortgage, but even then we do it out of love for those who depend on us. When we see a job as an act of love, it becomes more than a deadline met or an appliance assembled or a patient visited. It becomes a calling.

PRAY

Lord, help me notice today the small blessings in the out-of-the-way moments. Help my work today to be not only bearable but at least in modest ways enjoyable. Remind me of the people I help, the services I render, the pleasures I bring through what I do. And let me see how what I do can be an offering of love.

REMEMBER "It is not only prayer that gives God glory but work. Smiting on an anvil, sawing a beam, whitewashing a wall . . . sweeping, scouring . . . [God] is so great that all things give him glory if you mean [them to]" (Gerard Manley Hopkins, nineteenth century).[25]

A PRAYER TO KEEP ON KEEPING ON

"God is able to provide you with every blessing in abundance, so that by always having enough of everything, you may share abundantly in every good work" (2 Corinthians 9:8).

PRAY

Almighty God,
show us kindness
when we get bothered by what has happened
and lose faith and hope and courage.
So have mercy on us and help us that we,
sustained by confident faith that you forgive,
may go on in the life ahead of us
to keep your ways,
to rejoice in your blessings,
and to hope in the life to come.
Grant to all of us, whatever happens,
to remember that everything remains
under your will and guidance and care,
so that when things seem darkest,
we will see you and thereby have
courage to go forward,
faith to endure,
patience to keep on,
and hopefulness to hold out,
even to the end. Amen.

GEORGE DAWSON, NINETEENTH CENTURY, ADAPTED

REMEMBER Out of God's many resourceful abilities, he can supply you with courage to keep moving forward, even to the end.

SLIPPING INTO THE PRESENCE

The God Jesus revealed was a continual presence, closely involved in daily life, not a baffling deity enshrined on an unapproachable altar. . . . In the midst of [the] juggling act we daily live, prayer can become that place where we stand face-to-face with the most important realities, quaking and trembling perhaps, but nevertheless glad to be there. Prayer can be that sacred space where the real breaks in and we know unassailably that whoever else we may be, we are God's children, loved with a fierce and reckless abandon. What movement can be easier than slipping into the presence of the one who loves us?[26]

KATHY COFFEY

PRAY

O God, who lives and moves through the creation you have made, remind me that you long to draw close whenever I open my heart to you. Give me a deep and abiding willingness to entertain your merciful goodness in the moments of high worship as well as in the moments of the tasks I face today. Amen.

REMEMBER "In the rush and noise of life, as you have spaces, step within yourselves and be still. Wait upon God and feel his good presence; this will carry you through your day's business" (William Penn, seventeenth/eighteenth century).

ENLARGING YOUR REQUESTS

For many of us, prayer lapses into repetitions of things we are sure to ask for. We achieve a kind of perfunctory, customary patter—intercession for a sick aunt, help in paying the mortgage, release from a compulsive habit. But the range of ways God wants to bless our lives confounds the imagination. Let your prayers today encompass new and untried areas.

PRAY

O great God of heaven, draw my soul to you;
Give to me a sincere desire to be faithful.
O Healer of my soul, grant to me forgiveness;
Give to me joy and happiness.
O great God of life, breathe into me your life;
Give to me the Spirit's power.
O gracious God of angels, wash me in your light;
Give to me the loving spirit of Jesus the lamb.
TRADITIONAL CELTIC PRAYER, ADAPTED

REMEMBER "For as the heavens are higher than the earth [says the Lord], so are my ways higher than your ways and my thoughts than your thoughts" (Isaiah 55:9).

THE LIFE YOU'VE ALWAYS WANTED

Sometimes we battle a tired complacency that keeps us from growing. A boredom that shrinks the spirit. A dullness that keeps us from seeking God with our whole being. Wouldn't it be wonderful if it didn't need to be that way?

PRAY

Merciful God and mighty Lord,
were it not for your persistent, seeking love,
    I might delay in acting on your invitation to come.
Break through my hesitancy, I pray.

Help me today to keep you at the center of life,
    not on its edges.
Help my faith to throw itself into the fray
    and not stay content to sit on the sidelines.
Turn my wandering into readiness,
    my longings into faith,
        my doctrine into deeds.
I know that you wait to make my life
    into something it could never be
    without your empowering presence and grace. Amen.

REMEMBER "With God, go over the sea; without God, not over the threshold" (Russian proverb).

A PRAYER OF ST. FRANCIS

Often we come to God aware mostly of what God can do or give. Sometimes we need simply to approach God with praise for who he is.

PRAY

You are holy, Lord, the only God,
    and your deeds are wonderful.
You are strong, you are great.
You are the most High, you are Almighty.
You, holy Father, are King of heaven and earth.
You are three and one, Lord God.
You are good, all good, supreme good,
Lord God, living and true.
You are love, you are wisdom.
You are humility, you are endurance.
You are rest, you are peace.
You are joy and gladness,
    you are justice and moderation.
You are beauty, you are gentleness.
You are our protector, you are our
    guardian and defender.
You are courage, you are our haven
    and our hope.
You are our faith, our great consolation.
You are our eternal life, great and wonderful Lord,
God almighty, merciful Savior.[27]
ST. FRANCIS OF ASSISI, TWELFTH CENTURY

REMEMBER Throughout today let God's infinitely multifaceted character inspire you to praise and love.

TASTE AND SEE

We experience God not just through our minds but with every cell of our being as well. Our senses can become alert and alive to God's goodness.

PRAY

O God, help me go through life
*   with my senses on high alert.*
May everything and everyone draw my attention to you;
Grant me:
*   eyes to see the signs of your moving,*
*   ears to hear heavenly rumors of your marvels,*
*   fingers to touch earth's real-life wonders,*
*   a nose for the sweetness of your presence,*
*   a mouth that can taste and see that the Lord is good.*

REMEMBER "The mighty God, even the LORD, has spoken, and called the earth from the rising of the sun unto the going down thereof. Out of Zion, the perfection of beauty, God has shined" (Psalm 50:1–2, KJV, adapted).

AUTUMN

REST THAT RENEWS

Come to me, all you that are weary and are carrying heavy burdens, and I will give you rest. Take my yoke upon you, and learn from me; for I am gentle and humble in heart, and you will find rest for your souls. For my yoke is easy, and my burden is light.
JESUS, IN MATTHEW 11:28–30

PRAY

Lord, I often feel as though I'm not good at slowing down. Urgency to get things done drives me. I like too much to see things happen. No wonder I've become hurried and hassled and worn.

Draw me to the quiet strength I can find in your presence. Remind me that time with you can replenish my life and renew my work. Amen.

REMEMBER "O Lord, you know how busy I must be this day. If I forget you, please do not forget me" (Sir Jacob Asteley, sixteenth/seventeenth century).

A STILL POINT IN THE MOTION AND COMMOTION

Stress has become a buzzword of today's world. We feel frazzled and overwhelmed. Flurry and hurry become our twin perils. How do we survive—even thrive—in this storm of activity and demand? Prayer is always a good starting place.

PRAY

O Lord my God, be not far from me; take notice of me to help me, for distracting thoughts and great fears plague my soul. How can I pass through this time unhurt? . . . This is my hope, my one and only encouragement: to run to you in every hardship, to trust in you, to call on you from my inmost being, and to wait patiently for your comforting help.

ST. AUGUSTINE, FOURTH/FIFTH CENTURY, ADAPTED

REMEMBER "And while they were sailing [Jesus] fell asleep. A windstorm swept down on the lake, and the boat was filling with water, and they were in danger. They went to him and woke him up, shouting, 'Master, Master, we are perishing!' And he woke up and rebuked the wind and the raging waves; they ceased, and there was a calm" (Luke 8:23–24).

NEVER HASTY IN JUDGMENT

Occasions for taking offense are ever present. We tend quite easily to judge the motives of others, especially those who would hurt us. Prayer, however, injects another presence into our dark and sometimes vengeful thoughts. It brings light and life where our imaginations might lead us to wish ruin on others.

PRAY

Keep us, O God, from all pettiness.
Let us be large in thought, word, and deed.
> *Let us be done with fault finding*
>> *and leave off all self-seeking.*
May we put away all pretense
> *and meet each other face to face.*
May we never be hasty in judgment,
> *and always generous....*
Teach us to put into action our better impulses,
> *to be straightforward and unafraid.*

MARY STUART, SIXTEENTH CENTURY

REMEMBER "Therefore you have no excuse, whoever you are, when you judge others; for in passing judgment on another you condemn yourself, because you, the judge, are doing the very same things" (Romans 2:1).

NOT LOVING THE LIMELIGHT

No man appears in safety before the public eye unless he first relishes obscurity. No man is safe in speaking unless he loves to be silent. No man rules safely unless he is willing to be ruled. No man commands safely unless he has learned well how to obey. No man rejoices safely unless he has within him the testimony of a good conscience.

THOMAS À KEMPIS, FOURTEENTH/FIFTEENTH CENTURY

PRAY

Lord, you know that much in me prefers being noticed over noticing others. I would rather talk than listen. Too often I am quick to control and slow to give others room to move and breathe. Give me a new heart with those I work with today, a new openness to you, a new willingness to live not for myself.

REMEMBER While it may seem tough to let down our guard or relinquish control over others, there is ultimately great freedom in doing so. In the long run it gives God more opportunity to work and accomplish his purposes.

OUR NEED FOR WISDOM

As a culture we are awash in information. What generation has ever had at its fingertips (and at the click of a computer mouse) more data? We can get overwhelmed by the sheer volume of facts, news items, and things to know and remember. But what we know does not necessarily make us *wise*. We often feel informed but untransformed. We need more than reports and studies and figures. Something tells us it's time to go deeper, take time to think, make sure the day includes time to reflect. Only then will our knowledge do more than fill our heads.

PRAY

Lord, today I need more wisdom than I have. I have many items of information whirling around inside my head, but please let me see the significance of what I know. Allow me to do more than swallow numbers and regurgitate facts. Help me truly share with my colleagues words that illumine and instruct.

REMEMBER "For if you call on wisdom and knowledge with a loud voice, and seek it as treasures of silver, and eagerly track it out, you will understand godliness and find divine knowledge" (St. Clement of Alexandria, second/third century).

MORE THINGS THAN DREAMED

"There are more things in heaven and earth," said Shakespeare's Hamlet, "than are dreamt of in your philosophy." Sometimes all we see are inanimate objects: rocks, tables, windows. We allow our outlook to become limited by hard realities and daily circumstances. But within and behind and above, often without our knowing it, teems unseen celestial activity.

PRAY

Lord, help me sharpen my eyesight for the traces and signs of your glorious working. I may not see angelic realms or explosive miracles or the heavenly stratosphere. But remind me that your Spirit operates at all times, bursting the bounds of my categories.

REMEMBER "Beware in your prayer . . . of limiting God, not only by unbelief, [but] by fancying that you know what he can do" (Andrew Murray, nineteenth/twentieth century).[28]

THE ASSURANCE OF LOVE

There is no creature that is made that may [fully] know how much and how sweetly and how tenderly our Maker loves us. We may with grace and his help stand in spiritual beholding with everlasting marvel this high, surpassing, inestimable love that Almighty God shows to us in his goodness. And therefore we may ask of our Lover with reverence all that we will. For our natural will is to have God, and the good will of God is to have us.

DAME JULIAN OF NORWICH, FOURTEENTH/FIFTEENTH CENTURY, ADAPTED

PRAY

God, of your goodness, give me yourself,
for you are enough for me,
and I may ask nothing less that is worthy of you;
and if I ask anything less, I will always be wanting.
Only in you do I have all.

DAME JULIAN OF NORWICH, FOURTEENTH/FIFTEENTH CENTURY

REMEMBER "Our Lord God showed that it is very pleasing to him that a helpless soul come simply and plainly and humbly. For this is the natural yearning of the soul, through the touching of the Holy Spirit" (Dame Julian of Norwich, fourteenth/fifteenth century).

THE LIE ABOUT GIVING

It's easy, when pushed by the demands of our workplace, to feel that all we have time for is looking out for ourselves. Acting generously appears to be a luxury we cannot afford. But the wisest spiritual teachers remind us that God always graces our lives with enough to share. Because we are created to care, as we give we become the ones who gain.

PRAY

Lord, help me not to get so swept along by things to be done that I forget to notice people around me. Help me not to buy the lie that I have no time to care for those I work with. Give me a generous, more open heart. And let me learn once again the joys of helping another. Amen.

REMEMBER "You will be made rich in every way so that you can be generous on every occasion, and . . . your generosity will result in thanksgiving to God" (2 Corinthians 9:11, NIV).

THE STRUGGLE TO FORGIVE

"He has buried the hatchet," someone once said of a wronged man struggling to forgive. "But he made sure he left a marked grave." The struggles to forgive deep hurts are legendary—and no doubt real in your own life. While there are no tidy steps or easy solutions, praying about the wrong done—even praying for the one who did us wrong—rarely fails to help us.

PRAY

I offer up to you my prayers and intercessions, especially for those who in any way have hurt, grieved, or found fault with me—anyone who has done me damage or caused anger.

For those also whom at any time I may have irritated, troubled, burdened, and scandalized, by words or deeds, knowingly or in ignorance: grant us all equally forgiveness for our sins and our offenses against each other.

Take away from our hearts, O Lord, all suspiciousness, indignation, wrath, and contention, and whatever may chip away compassion and diminish love.

Have mercy, O Lord, have mercy on those who long for your mercy; give grace to those that stand in need of it. Amen.

THOMAS À KEMPIS, FOURTEENTH/FIFTEENTH CENTURY

REMEMBER Along with all your efforts to forgive those who have hurt you, never neglect prayer. Always be ready to turn to a God who is an expert in forgiveness.

THE WORLD AROUND ME

It may be difficult in your workplace to remember the world that God has created. But all that is around us—whether concrete and glass or woods and lakes—exists by the hand of the universe's creator. Pause now to look up and look around. Allow yourself to take in the goodness of creation. Take a moment to breathe thanks to the One who made it.

PRAY

The heavens are telling the glory of God;
*   and the firmament proclaims his handiwork.*
Day to day pours forth speech,
*   and night to night declares knowledge.*

PSALM 19:1–2

REMEMBER "Wherever you cast your eyes, there is no spot in the universe wherein you cannot discern at least some sparks of [God's] glory" (John Calvin, sixteenth century).

A RECEIVING FRAME OF MIND AND HEART

God does not demand from us absolute strength, just a heart open to him.

PRAY

Behold, Lord, an empty vessel that needs to be filled.
My Lord, fill it.
I am weak in the faith;
strengthen me.
I am cold in love;
warm me and make me fervent,
that my love may go out to my neighbor.
O Lord, help me.
Strengthen my faith and trust in you.
In you I have sealed the treasure of all I have.
I am poor;
you are rich.
I am a sinner;
you are upright.
With me, there is an abundance of sin;
in you is the fullness of righteousness.
Therefore I will remain in you,
of whom I can receive,
but to whom I may not give.

MARTIN LUTHER, FIFTEENTH/SIXTEENTH CENTURY

REMEMBER When we fall on our knees in dependence, we will stand up in strength.

THE GREATEST LINK

We sometimes imagine that what we do matters far more than how we pray or even *that* we pray. How mistaken! Prayer links our little lives with creation's God and the universe's maker and mover. Prayer, then, is no vaguely pious sentiment, but the opening of our lives to an infinite and influential presence.

PRAY

Answer me when I call, O God of my right!
You gave me room when I was in distress.
Be gracious to me, and hear my prayer....
There are many who say, "O that we might see some good!
Let the light of your face shine on us, O LORD!"
You have put gladness in my heart
more than when their grain and wine abound.
I will both lie down and sleep in peace;
for you alone, O LORD, make me lie down in safety.

PSALM 4:1, 6–8

REMEMBER Prayer links our little lives with creation's God and the universe's maker and mover.

BREATH NEVER SPENT IN VAIN

No prayer is lost. Praying breath was never spent in vain. There is no such thing as prayer unanswered or unnoticed by God, and some things that we count refusals or denials are simply delays.

HORATIUS BONAR, NINETEENTH CENTURY

PRAY

Lord, I want to pray regularly and faithfully, but I wonder sometimes if I get through to you. I strain to see answers that I fear will never materialize, and then it becomes hard to wait. Remind me to pray not only with hope but also with patience. I want to come to you with more than urgency, with trust too. Help me see the longer view, the answers seen with eyes grown sharper through love and faith. In the name of One who trusted you for everything, in life and in death. Amen.

REMEMBER God is a prayer-hearing God. God likes to hear us talk. He wants us to seek him and then make room for his answers.

PRAYER ON THE RUN

On a day of traveling—with, perhaps, some ghastly meeting at the end of it—I'd rather pray sitting in a crowded train than put it off till midnight when one reaches a hotel bedroom with aching head and dry throat and one's mind partly in a stupor and partly in a whirl. On other, and slightly less crowded, days a bench in a park, or a back street where one can pace up and down, will do.[29]

C. S. LEWIS, TWENTIETH CENTURY

PRAY

Lord, you know the little details of my life, my comings and goings, my frantic times and still moments. Help me remember you, wherever I am, whatever I'm doing. I want to become more than a person who prays, but a person formed and shaped and deepened by prayer in every way.

REMEMBER "May the Lord of peace himself give you peace at all times and in every way. The Lord be with you all" (2 Thessalonians 3:16, NJB).

THE GOD OF THE PURSUIT

I fled Him, down the night and down the day;
   I fled Him, down the arches of the years;
I fled Him, down the labyrinthine ways
   Of my own mind; and in the mist of tears
I hid from Him, and under running laughter.
   Up vistaed hopes I sped;
   And shot, precipitated,
Adown Titanic glooms of chasmed fears,
   From those strong Feet that followed, followed after.
   But with unhurrying chase,
   And unperturbed pace
Deliberate speed, majestic instancy,
   They beat—and a Voice beat
   more instant than the Feet—
"All things betray thee, who betrayest Me."

FRANCIS THOMPSON, NINETEENTH CENTURY

PRAY

Bring us, O Lord God, at the last awakening into the house and gate of heaven, to enter that gate and dwell in that house, where there shall be no darkness nor dazzling, but one equal light; no fears nor hopes, but an equal procession; no ends nor beginnings, but one equal eternity, in the habitations of your majesty and glory, world without end.

JOHN DONNE, SIXTEENTH/SEVENTEENTH CENTURY

REMEMBER How wonderful to know that, with all our searching, God was already seeking, long before us!

WINGS OF FREEDOM

In a time when many are discovering the need for appropriate assertiveness, we may forget the value of laying down our wants and rights. We are so likely to emphasize "following our own bliss" that we forget the profound power of offering our life in the service of God and others. But in freedom's paradox, we find ourselves only as we do what we are made to do: worship and serve God.

PRAY

The chains you place on me, O Lord, are the wings of freedom. There is no liberty like the liberty of being bound in service, ready to go. When you lay on me a sense of obligation, you in that moment set me free. When you say that I must, my heart says, "I can."...

Bind me to yourself as you bind planets to the sun, that it may become the very law of my nature to be led by you. May I content myself in knowing that goodness and mercy shall follow me without waiting to see them in advance of me.
GEORGE MATHESON, NINETEENTH CENTURY, ADAPTED

REMEMBER "I appeal to you . . . brothers and sisters, by the mercies of God, to present your bodies as a living sacrifice, holy and acceptable to God, which is your spiritual worship" (Romans 12:1).

A LABOR NOT IN VAIN

It doesn't take many years of experience to discover that life is not always a pleasant stroll. Faithfulness demands more of us than occasional dabbling or mild curiosity. Only perseverance will get us through. Be sure today to ask God for all the help you need to keep on keeping on.

PRAY

Most merciful Lord, grant to me your grace, that it will go with me, and work with me, and persevere with me to the very end. Grant that I may always desire and will that which is to you most acceptable and pleasing. Let your will be mine, and my will ever follow yours, and agree with it completely. Grant to me, above all things that can be desired, to rest in you, and in you to have my heart at peace. You are the true peace of the heart, you its only rest, and outside of you all things are hard and restless.
THOMAS À KEMPIS, FOURTEENTH/FIFTEENTH CENTURY

REMEMBER "Therefore . . . be steadfast, immovable, always excelling in the work of the Lord, because you know that in the Lord your labor is not in vain" (1 Corinthians 15:58).

COME TO THE QUIET

Come now . . .
turn aside for a while from your daily work.
Escape for a minute from the turmoil of your thoughts.
Put aside your worries.
Let your burdensome distractions wait.
Free yourself for a while for God and rest for a time in him.
Enter the interior room of your soul and shut out everything
but God
and that will help you in looking for him.
When you have shut the door, look for him.
Look with your whole heart.
ST. ANSELM, ELEVENTH CENTURY, ADAPTED

PRAY

Lord, help me now to pray in quiet,
not worrying about the words,
only sitting still in your presence,
until it is time to move on.

REMEMBER Half the battle in prayer is sitting still long enough
to ask, receive, and listen.

A TONIC FOR TIRED SOULS

Just as our bodies get weary, our souls may grow tired and unable to feel much. We get spiritually sluggish. We sleepwalk through the simple glories of everyday life. We wonder if we can shake loose from our spiritual dormancy to notice again creation's wonders or life's everyday miracles.

PRAY

Please, Lord, help me not yawn my way through another day of hidden glories and small breakthroughs. Give me a wakeful heart. Amen.

REMEMBER "Be careful then how you live, not as unwise people but as wise, making the most of the time, because the days are evil" (Ephesians 5:15).

GOING DEEPER

"A mile wide but only an inch deep." That was the expression someone once used for a shallow faith.

In what ways may God be calling you to go deeper in your times of prayer and your expressions of daily faithfulness?

Ask God now for guidance and courage not to settle for the superficial. Ask God to take you deeper.

PRAY

Lord, teach me to quiet my heart
that I may listen to the gentle movement
of the Holy Spirit within me
and sense the depths that are of God.
ELIJAH DE VIDAS, SIXTEENTH CENTURY, ADAPTED

REMEMBER How beyond our imagining is God in all his radiant splendor. Yet God invites us to try.

STANDING READY TO LISTEN

The LORD called [the boy] Samuel . . . and Samuel got up [from his bed] and went to [the temple priest, his mentor and guardian] Eli and said, "Here I am; you called me."

Then Eli realized that the LORD was calling the boy. So Eli told Samuel, "Go and lie down, and if he calls you, say, 'Speak, LORD, for your servant is listening.'" So Samuel went and lay down in his place.

1 SAMUEL 3:8–9, NIV

PRAY

Lord, teach me to listen. The times are noisy and my ears are weary with the thousand raucous sounds which continuously assault them. Give me the spirit of the boy Samuel when he said to Thee, "Speak, for thy servant heareth." Let me hear Thee speaking in my heart. Let me get used to the sound of Thy voice, that its tones may be familiar when the sounds of earth die away and the only sound will be the music of Thy speaking voice.[30]

A. W. TOZER, TWENTIETH CENTURY

REMEMBER God communicates continuously, through a host of ways and means. Take time today, if only a few minutes, to ask God for guidance.

WHO STILLS THE SOUL?

Be still, my soul: your God will undertake
To guide the future, as he has the past.
Your hope, your confidence let nothing shake;
All now mysterious shall be bright at last.
Be still, my soul: the waves and winds shall know
His voice who ruled them while he dwelt below.
KATHARINA VON SCHLEGE, EIGHTEENTH CENTURY

PRAY

Lord, I need assurance as I think of what has gone before and what stretches ahead. I feel regret for what has been done and left undone. I struggle with anxiety for things to come I cannot control or guarantee. Let me find, in this present moment, the grace to trust you with what has been and the courage to believe that all will eventually be well. Amen.

REMEMBER While we don't know what tomorrow holds, we know that God holds tomorrow.

NOTICING THE GLORIES

"Pied Beauty"

Glory to God for dappled things—

    For skies of couple-color as a brindled cow;

        For rose-moles all in stipple upon trout that swim;

Fresh-firecoal chestnut-falls; finches' wings;

    Landscape plotted and pieced—fold, fallow, and plough;

        And all trades, their gear and tackle and trim.

All things counter, original, spare, strange;

    Whatever is fickle, freckled, (who knows how?)

        With swift, slow; sweet, sour; adazzle, dim;

He fathers-forth whose beauty is past change:

        Praise him.

GERARD MANLEY HOPKINS, NINETEENTH CENTURY

PRAY

Lord, what a wonder is the world you have made! Give me eyes to see, ears to hear, skin to sense, that I may not pass by the wonders you leave standing all around, hidden in plain sight. Amen.

REMEMBER Ask God to open your soul to divine wonders today, so that you do not miss the glories that you sometimes rush by.

GOD AS MY VISION

Corporate consultants often bandy about the word *vision* when trying to help companies chart a new course. A vision, they know, can marshal energy and guide a group to its true destination.

In your daily life how might God become more and more the source and substance of your vision?

PRAY

Be Thou my Vision, O Lord of my heart;
Naught be all else to me, save that Thou art
Thou my best Thought, by day or by night,
Waking or sleeping, Thy presence my light.

Be Thou my battle Shield, Sword for the fight;
Be Thou my Dignity, Thou my Delight;
Thou my soul's Shelter, Thou my high Tower:
Raise Thou me heavenward, O Power of my power.

Riches I heed not, nor others' empty praise,
Thou mine Inheritance, now and always:
Thou and Thou only, first in my heart,
High King of heaven, my Treasure Thou art.

High King of heaven, my victory won,
May I reach heaven's joys, O bright heaven's Sun!
Heart of my own heart, whatever befall,
Still be my Vision, O Ruler of all.

TRANSLATED FROM ANCIENT IRISH TO ENGLISH BY MARY ELIZABETH BYRNE, TWENTIETH CENTURY

REMEMBER "Where there is no vision, the people perish" (Proverbs 29:18, KJV).

AVOIDING SHORTCUT PRAYERS

Don't pray for tasks equal to your powers. Pray for powers
equal to your tasks.

PHILLIPS BROOKS, NINETEENTH CENTURY

PRAY

*O Lord, we earnestly ask you that your people would grow ever
in love toward you, their Father who is in heaven, and may so be
taught by the example of holy deeds, that they would always, as
you pour your gifts upon them, walk before you in all such
things as would be well-pleasing in the sight of your divine
majesty.*

ROMAN BREVIARY, ADAPTED

REMEMBER We do not pray in order to have an easy life, but a
faithful one.

WHAT'S OBVIOUS, WHAT'S NOT

Do you sometimes wonder if your efforts to do good only get lost in a whirl of workplace activity? Perhaps you fear that your attempts to follow Christ's example go unnoticed, blending into the vast monotony of a world hell-bent on profit and productivity.

But the testimony of our wisest spiritual teachers confirms that the littlest act carries unseen repercussions. We are never *not* demonstrating what we believe to others, through what we say and do and choose not to. We are never *not* bearing witness to the presence of good within us or to the influence of evil.

PRAY

Lord, I choose to believe that even small gestures carry weight. When my conviction sags, remind me that you took a ragtag band of first-century followers of Jesus and changed the course of history. Help me to serve even when there is no sight of impact or change. Allow me to stay faithful no matter what. Amen.

REMEMBER "The sins of some people are conspicuous and precede them to judgment, while the sins of others follow them there. So also good works are conspicuous; and even when they are not, they cannot remain hidden" (1 Timothy 5:24–25).

THE GOOD NEWS
ABOUT WHAT LASTS

We live in an age of acceleration, a time of great mobility. Events move quickly, and people pass in and out of our lives. What seemed stable and sure yesterday lands today in a dustbin, a victim of innovation and "improvement." Things never stop passing away. Indeed, there is a transitory nature to nearly everything we enjoy. We don't need to be depressed about this. Whatever is truly important also happens to last forever.

PRAY

Lord, remind me of the ways in which you go on through eternity. When I am tempted to despair over things I cannot keep, over experiences I cannot box up, over relationships I cannot capture in a freeze-frame, remind me that you are gracious and good and eternal.

REMEMBER "The grass withers, the flower fades; but the word of our God will stand forever" (Isaiah 40:8).

MORE THAN WORDS

Prayer crowns God with the honor and glory due his name, and God crowns prayer with assurance and comfort. The most praying souls are the most assured souls.

THOMAS BENTON BROOKS, SEVENTEENTH CENTURY

PRAY

Lord, as I pray today, let me do more than mouth the words; let me see in my mind's eye your tangible reality, your glorious power, your great compassion. Let me give you your due, not only in my words, but also in my attitude—toward you and toward others. Amen.

REMEMBER "This is the confidence that we have in him, that, if we ask any thing according to his will, he heareth us" (1 John 5:14, KJV).

WHEN LIFE SEEMS ELOQUENT

Life speaks with a certain eloquence, if we learn to listen. Often the wisdom we need, the guidance we seek, or the meaning we long for can be found more or less by prayerfully paying attention. Growing spiritually happens in similarly typical settings. We learn amid everyday life's signals and signposts, amid the holy and even horrible turns.

PRAY

Gracious Lord, full of wisdom and willingness to communicate, help me not be dense or deliberately hard of hearing. If already you are speaking and leading and acting, unstop my ears. I need your help in not missing your voice, which whispers and calls me right where I am, right where I live.

REMEMBER "Let your life speak" (Quaker proverb).

PREDESTINED FOR FREEDOM

Someone pondering the mysteries of destiny once asked a philosopher, "Do you believe in free will?" "Of course," came the reply. "We have no other choice!" You don't have to be a determinist to know that life does not rest on pure chance.

In what ways can you, with free heart and loving submission, let God enlist you in vast, eternal plans?

PRAY
Our Father,
Your will be done on earth, as it is in heaven.
Amen.

REMEMBER God works in daily circumstances, unfolding his purposes, inviting us to cooperate with him in the choices we make and the prayers we say.

STARTING RIGHT, FINISHING WELL

No runner wants merely to *start* a race. There is an undeniable urge to make it to the finish line. We begin any enterprise with a desire to see our efforts brought to a good conclusion. This is just as true with the life of faith. Fortunately, we are not alone. God comes alongside and keeps us going, even when we would grow tired.

PRAY

O Lord God, when you allow and prompt your servants to attempt any great matter, remind us that it is not the beginning, but the continuing of it—until it is completely finished—that yields the true glory; through him that for the finishing of your work laid down his life, our Redeemer, Jesus Christ. Amen.

SIR FRANCIS DRAKE, SIXTEENTH CENTURY, ADAPTED

REMEMBER When it becomes hard to continue, never hesitate to turn to God for renewed conviction, courage, and strength. "I am confident of this, that the one who began a good work among you will bring it to completion by the day of Jesus Christ" (Philippians 1:6).

NO DOUBT ABOUT FORGIVENESS

Few things hold us back from a vital expectancy around God as the nagging doubt that we may have offended him. That lingering old business from our mistakes will cloud our freedom as believers. How can standing on God's scriptural promises to forgive lead you to a new joy?

PRAY

Almighty and most merciful God,
> *in whom we live, and move, and have our being;*
Lord of all life,
>> *Source of all light,*
>>> *guiding and governing all things*
>>>> *with your loving kindness and power.*
Hear our thanksgivings to you for all the joy you put into everyday life
>> *and especially for the joy that comes of sin forgiven,*
>>> *weakness strengthened,*
>>>> *victory promised,*
>>>>> *eternal life looked for.*
Grant that, being fully aware of having erred and wandered from your ways,
>> *we would be just as aware of our need*
>>> *to go back again to the Good Shepherd.*
Let there be no doubt that you forgive—completely—all those who come to you;
>> *so we who are sinful, and sad because of it,*
may experience today the joy of the Lord.

GEORGE DAWSON, NINETEENTH CENTURY, ADAPTED

REMEMBER "There is forgiveness with you [O Lord], so that you may be revered" (Psalm 130:4).

OPENING OUR HANDS

Sometimes we grab and grasp our way through our circumstances. We have trouble holding things lightly—despite life's constant lesson that many things do best when given freedom to blossom without our supervision. In letting go, however, we often find our truest, most natural relationship to the things we think we should manipulate.

PRAY

Lord, I want to open my life to you and your gracious work. You are wonderful and wondrously able. Help me loosen my grip on what I hold too tightly. Allow me to trust you with the many details I tend to clutch and worry over. Lead me forward into that placid place where I cease my striving and allow you all the room you want to accomplish your purposes. Amen.

REMEMBER "When in prayer you clasp your hands, God opens his" (German proverb).

THE ATTITUDE OF GRATITUDE

Someone once told a friend he wanted to cultivate an "attitude of gratitude." He had decided that he didn't want to be plagued by whining. He wanted to be buoyed by alert, thankful awareness of all that God was bringing about.

This attitude shift is not easy. But developing a healthy outlook or a new habit always requires effort and attention.

PRAY

I deeply want, O God, this day to please you; to do your will in all the things you give me to do; to bear each thing you allow to happen to me contrary to my will, meekly, humbly, patiently, as a gift from you to subdue self-will in me; and to make your will wholly mine.... May I thank you, if not in words, yet in my heart, for each gift of your love, for each comfort that you provide day by day. Amen.

E. B. PUSEY, NINETEENTH CENTURY, ADAPTED

REMEMBER "The best way to show my gratitude to God is to accept everything, even my problems, with joy" (Mother Teresa of Calcutta, twentieth century).[31]

THE POWER OF NOT DOING

We tend to measure our lives by how many successes we rack up, how many goals and ambitions we fulfill. "What do you do for a living?" we ask someone we are first getting to know. We put the accent on action, movement, progress. Rarely do we pause to sit back and enjoy life as it is.

What are some ways you can practice the discipline of slowing down this week? How can you make room for the joys of simply being and not overrate the lure of always doing?

PRAY

Lord, let me not be so caught up in a drive to get things done that I neglect to enjoy you and the countless blessings you have scattered throughout my life. Allow me to open up the too-busy parts of my life to discover your free and refreshing and unfrantic way of being.

REMEMBER "Be still, and know that I am God! I am exalted among the nations, I am exalted in the earth" (Psalm 46:10).

NOT BEING USELESS

We are tempted to think that the most satisfying life comes from minding our own business and tending our need for personal security. But testimony from our spiritual forebears tells us again and again that the greatest joy comes from throwing away our own self-absorbed quests. We deepen and enrich life as we care for others and learn to love generously.

How can your prayers today take you out of yourself and orient you to the ways you can help and serve others?

PRAY

O Lord, let me not live to be useless.

JOHN WESLEY, EIGHTEENTH CENTURY

REMEMBER "With the knowledge of God comes love" (St. Catherine of Siena, fourteenth century).

THE IMPOSSIBILITY
OF LOVING OTHERS

As anyone who has tried to love an unlovable person can attest, few things seem as impossible and beyond earthly ability. In a way, that recognition leads to a profound discovery: Love has to do with more than human resolve or earnest effort. Loving by our own inclinations cannot take us far. No wonder the New Testament rarely tells us to love others without first reminding us that God loves us. Loving when it gets tough grows out of God's freeing, enabling concern for us. When we feel valued by God, we are most able to give, share, and sacrifice; then we have a full heart that allows us to share the most generously. We give what we, in a sense, have already been given.

PRAY

Lord, I need your grace and peace to save me from my sputtering efforts. Your loving presence brings into my life something I cannot muster on my own. Your cross is the offer of a love that can fill me with love that lets me reach out in compassion as never before. Amen.

REMEMBER "There is an Arm that never tires, / When human strength gives way" (George Matheson, nineteenth century).

"It is ours to offer what we can, God's to supply what we cannot" (St. Jerome, fourth/fifth century).

THE CHARACTER OF LOVE

Every love has its own force; and it cannot lie inactive in the soul of the one who loves. Love must draw the soul on. Do you wish to know the character of a love? Well, see where it leads.
ST. AUGUSTINE, FOURTH/FIFTH CENTURY, ADAPTED

PRAY

Lord, may my heart be open to those who require an extra measure of caring today. I know how prone to impatience or criticism I can be. Please allow your love, planted in me, to draw me out of my petty concerns and insensitivity.

REMEMBER "No cord or cable can draw so forcibly, or bind so fast, as love can do with a single thread" (Robert Burton, sixteenth/seventeenth century).

THE AWFUL POWER OF ENVY

Are there ways in which envy is distracting you, perhaps even eating away at your life? Prayerfully ask God to show how envy creeps into your relationships at work: Perhaps you resent someone's promotion, looks, income, or friends.

PRAY

Lord, let your soothing, healing, cleansing Spirit wash across our bruised and battered lives. Take away all that festers and spoils within—all envy, discontent, all malice, every jealous thought. And teach us the true meaning of contentment based in your love. Reveal to us the way to peace, that peace that passes understanding.[32]

J. BARRIE SHEPHERD

REMEMBER "Envy is like a disease—it consumes the soul" (Jewish proverb).

WHAT LOVE LOOKS LIKE

What does love look like?

It has hands to help others.

It has feet to move us to the poor and needy.

It has eyes to see suffering and need.

It has ears to hear the sighs and sorrows of
others. That is what love looks like.

ST. AUGUSTINE, FOURTH/FIFTH CENTURY, ADAPTED

PRAY

*Lord, I can guess I will meet someone today who needs a work of
kindness or a word of sympathy. Keep me from hesitating when
what I can do comes into view. Allow me to carry on my job
while offering small gestures or kind words to those I work with
and those I will talk with when I head home. Amen.*

REMEMBER Love looks surprisingly daily, even dull, when it
works itself out in our relationships.

THE PEOPLE WE WORRY ABOUT

It is natural to worry about others—friends, colleagues, family—who struggle or wander or face harrowing experiences. Some days we even have trouble getting them off our minds.

Compassion finds in prayer a wonderful outlet at such times.

PRAY

Deliver the prisoner;   rescue the distressed;

Feed the hungry;   comfort the weak-hearted,

Convert the erring;   enlighten the darkened;

Raise the fallen; strengthen the wavering; heal the sick;

And guide them all, good Lord, into the way of salvation,

And into your sacred fold.

Deliver us, too, from our sins;

Protect and defend us at all times.

LITURGY OF ST. MARK, SECOND TO FIFTH CENTURIES, ADAPTED

REMEMBER We don't pray instead of offering our help, of course, but we also let our concern become energy for diligent prayer, seeking for others what often only God can provide.

FIERY PRAYER

Praying never requires us to become passive or automatic. Healthy, wholesome prayer, like that found in the Bible and in history's profoundest prayers, often assumes a lively, even fiery, quality. It may have an edge to it. It certainly does not greet injustice or wrongdoing with a placid smile or a grain of tolerant salt.

Are your prayers too modest, too quiet, too complacent?

PRAY

How long, O Lord? Will you forget me forever?
How long will you hide your face from me?
How long must I wrestle with my thoughts
and every day have sorrow in my heart?
How long will my enemy triumph over me?

PSALM 13:1–2, NIV

REMEMBER Prayer is a kind of protest against the way things are. It dares us to believe that another reality is possible, even necessary, for others, for ourselves.

KEEP IT REAL

Much can happen in prayer when we give up trying to bluster and pretend. We face honest shortcomings and, confronting them squarely, ask for help in finding another way.

PRAY

Lord, may my prayer today be more than a rote duty,
    but an honest seeking,
    a heartfelt encounter,
    an eager adventure.

Make me restless for your Spirit's genuine presence
    that I might not settle for anything fake or dishonest.

Please lead me deeper into all truth and give me the courage to
accept it. Amen.

REMEMBER Let your prayer today be real, not processed or disguised. Take the risk of going deeper and telling God where you are, what you feel.

THE SIMPLE WAY TO RICH PRAYER

Someone once asked a spiritual guide how to have a richer prayer life. The wise woman's advice was simple: Take the short prayer Jesus taught his disciples (known to many as the Lord's Prayer or Our Father) "but take an hour to say it."

Perhaps you do not have an hour now, but the compact prayer Jesus gave his followers (see Matthew 6:9–13 and Luke 11:2–4) can provide a rich outline of prayer for whatever time you do have.

PRAY

Our Father which art in heaven,
Hallowed be thy name.
Thy kingdom come.
Thy will be done in earth, as it is in heaven.
Give us this day our daily bread.
And forgive us our debts, as we forgive our debtors.
And lead us not into temptation, but deliver us from evil:
For thine is the kingdom, and the power, and the glory, for ever.
Amen.

JESUS, IN MATTHEW 6:9–13, KJV

REMEMBER Let the phrases of the Lord's Prayer serve as prayer starters for you as you personalize them and include details relevant to your own life and longings.

STANDING BACK
FROM THE DEMANDS

Every now and then it is good to stand back from the daily demands and look at our commitments prayerfully. Do our tasks and commitments assume an appropriate place in our lives? This week are we working honestly, conscientiously? On the other hand, are we making our job or others' demands so huge that we verge on burnout? Asking such questions in the presence of God may be the most important thing you can do on the job today.

PRAY

Lord, help me love my work but not be enslaved by it. Help me want to do it well but not allow it to consume my life. I want to faithfully do what is mine to do but not assume responsibilities I cannot and should not take on.

REMEMBER Let the thoughts of the psalmist guide your words and thoughts and prayers today on the job:

"Show me your ways, O Lord, teach me your paths; guide me in your truth and teach me, for you are God my Savior, and my hope is in you all day long" (Psalm 25:4–5, NIV).

THE COMMAND TO REST

Weariness often surrounds our thoughts of work. Sometimes our fatigue extends to all areas of life: household chores, days off, family outings, even our relationship with God. At such times it helps to remember that God does not expect us to work and stay on guard constantly; in the Bible God often tells—commands—his people to enjoy rest. God promises that such times can renew and refresh and make us better able to carry out his purposes. At a harrowing time for the people of Israel, God promises Moses, "I myself shall go with you and I shall give you rest" (Exodus 33:14, NJB).

PRAY

Do not tire of me, good Lord, and let me not tire of you. I am weak, but you are strong; you can display your strength perfectly in my weakness.[33]

E. B. PUSEY, NINETEENTH CENTURY, ADAPTED

REMEMBER "Take rest; a field that has rested gives a bountiful crop" (Ovid, first century B.C.).

MAKING MUSIC

"Life is like music," said the nineteenth-century writer Samuel Butler. "It must be composed by ear, feeling, and instinct, not by rule."

Our daily activities likewise can be composed and ordered not just by the rigid demands of schedule or stress but also by the gentle cadences of inner music. We can join in the harmonies of creation. Are there ways you can approach the tasks and demands of today with at least a snatch of a song stirring your heart and soul?

PRAY

Lord, today I need more than technique or smarts. I need a sanctified creativity to go through all of my duties. Help me sense the melodies hidden in the ordinary moments, the everyday chores. May I be your instrument and your voice. Amen.

REMEMBER "One is scarcely sensible of fatigue while he or she marches to music" (Thomas Carlyle, nineteenth century).

NO DEED TOO SMALL

Are we usually aware of how significant our words and deeds really are? We suspect that our deeds hardly matter, especially when flung in the faces of worldwide suffering, war, and famine. But we forget that God can use what we do in ways we cannot see. God can invest our little acts with a carrying power beyond our range of vision. And God can inhabit our small, faithful efforts with his own hidden power.

PRAY

Teach me, my God and King,
In all things thee to see,
And what I do in any thing,
to do it as for thee.
GEORGE HERBERT, SEVENTEENTH CENTURY

REMEMBER "There is nothing small in the service of God" (St. Francis de Sales, sixteenth/seventeenth century).

EMPATHY FOR OUR COLLEAGUES

Sometimes we get so caught up in our job descriptions that we brush past deeply hurting people in our workplaces. We may not be equipped to counsel, our time may not allow us to drop everything, and there may be some limits to how much we help.

PRAY

Loving and tenderhearted Father in heaven, I confess with sorrow how hard and unsympathetic is my heart, how often I have sinned against those around me by lack of compassion and tenderness, how often I have felt no empathy for another's hardships and sadnesses, and have neglected to help or visit or console....

Give me grace regularly to offer help for the difficulties of those I see, and never to add to them. Teach me how to wisely encourage, to care for the unknown person who needs my help, to care for the widow and orphan and divorcée.

Let my compassion show itself not only in words but also in action and truth. Amen.

JOHANN ARND, SIXTEENTH/SEVENTEENTH CENTURY, ADAPTED

REMEMBER So many people would be encouraged by our simply noticing their pain and offering a small gesture or a kind word—and perhaps even a prayer!

A PRAYER FOR GUIDANCE

Someone has said that if you have no goal, it's a guarantee that you will never arrive. Likewise, if we never seek guidance from God, it's no wonder life gets more confusing.

PRAY

O Creator beyond all words,
you have appointed from the riches of your wisdom
the ranks of angels,
disposing them in wondrous order above the bright heavens,
and have so beautifully set out all parts of the universe.

You we call the true source of wisdom
and the admirable origin of all things.
Be pleased to shed on the darkness of mind in which I was born,
The beams of both your light and warmth
to dispel my ignorance and sin.

You who can make eloquent the words of children
Instruct my speech and touch my lips with graciousness.
Make me eager to understand,
quick to learn,
able to remember;
make me delicate to interpret and ready to speak.

Guide my coming in and going forward,
lead home my going out.
You are true God and true human,
and live for ever and ever.

ST. THOMAS AQUINAS, THIRTEENTH CENTURY, ADAPTED

REMEMBER The God who lives forever and sees our coming and going is infinitely able—and eminently available—to lead us in the ways we should walk.

THE SHEPHERD
OF THE WORKPLACE

Every job, no matter how surrounded by the busyness of colleagues and constant motion, has its lonely moments. The isolated tedium of a task, the anxiety of making a crucial decision, or the threat of rupture in workplace relationships can make us feel keenly that we do our jobs on our own.

PRAY

The Lord is my shepherd;
*   I shall not want.*
He makes me to lie down in green pastures:
*   he leads me beside the still waters.*
He restores my soul:
*   he leads me in the paths of righteousness for his name's sake.*
Yes, though I walk through the valley of the shadow of death,
*   I will fear no evil:*
*   for you are with me; your rod and your staff comfort me.*
You prepare a table before me in the presence of mine enemies:
You anoint my head with oil;
*   my cup runs over.*
Surely goodness and mercy shall follow me all the days of
my life:
*   and I will dwell in the house of the Lord for ever.*

PSALM 23, KJV, ADAPTED

REMEMBER As we commit our lives to a gentle Guide and loving Shepherd, he promises to accompany us through every turn in the path, every danger along the way.

GOD'S HELP FOR STRESS

In proper doses, stress prompts us to do what we need to get done but prefer to put off. But more often than not, stress eats away at our inner well-being. It may wreak telltale symptoms in our bodies. This kind of stress can seem impossible to shake. But we can let it drive us to prayer, where we can find the calm and the nerve to face all our pressures and worries.

PRAY

Give me, O Lord, a steadfast heart,
*   which no unworthy affection may drag downward.*
Give me an unconquered heart,
*   which no tribulation can wear out.*
Give me an upright heart,
*   which no unworthy purpose may tempt aside.*
Bestow on me also, O Lord my God,
*   understanding to know you,*
*   diligence to find you,*
*   and a faithfulness that may finally embrace you,*
through Jesus Christ our Lord, Amen.[34]

ST. THOMAS AQUINAS, THIRTEENTH CENTURY

REMEMBER Perhaps nothing helps us with daily stresses as much as an active prayer life.

A NEEDED INVITATION

God is eager to be a part of our daily lives, but sometimes he waits for our invitation. Have you invited God into your decisions, your struggles, your opportunities today?

PRAY

Come, my Way, my Truth, my Life:
Such a Way, as gives us breath:
Such a Truth, as ends all strife:
And such a Life, as killeth death.

Come, my Joy, my Love, my Heart:
Such a Joy, as none can move:
Such a Love, as none can part:
Such a Heart, as delights in love.

GEORGE HERBERT, SEVENTEENTH CENTURY

REMEMBER When Jesus called himself the Way, the Truth, and the Life, he employed not only theological terms but also very personal promises.

WHAT NAME SHALL I CALL YOU?

Prayer can take on an easy familiarity. That is as it should be. But we also need a reverence that originates in a God mysterious and beyond easy grasp.

PRAY

O transcendent, almighty God,
What words can sing your praises?
No tongue can describe you.
No mind can probe your mystery.
Yet all speech springs from you,
And all thought stems from you.
All creation speaks of you,
All creatures reverence you. . . .
All things are upheld by you.
And they move according to your pleasing design.
The whole world longs for you,
And all people want you.
Yet you have set yourself apart,
You are well beyond our grasp.
You are the goal of all that exists,
But you do not let us comprehend you.
Lord, I want to speak to you.
By what name shall I call you?[35]

ST. GREGORY OF NAZIANZUS, FOURTH CENTURY, ADAPTED

REMEMBER Sometimes our prayers need to ask God questions and pave the way for God to come with new answers.

STRENGTH WHEN WEAK

Are you tempted to hide your weaknesses? Most of us don't relish revealing our sadness or fears or shortcomings. But our weaknesses often provide the very places where God's strength can become all the more evident.

PRAY

Almighty and merciful God,
our strength when we feel weak,
our refreshment when tired,
our encouragement when sad,
our help when tempted,
our life when facing our mortality,
the God of all patience and comfort,

Help me to attend to my soul in patience,
to maintain unshaken hope in you,
to keep that childlike trust that feels a Father's heart hidden
in hardship.
May I be strengthened with your wonderful divine power
so that I can endure hurt and suffering
and in the very depth of my suffering
praise you with a joyful heart.

JOHANN HABERMANN, SIXTEENTH CENTURY, ADAPTED

REMEMBER "But [God] said to me, 'My grace is sufficient for you, for power is made perfect in weakness'" (2 Corinthians 12:9).

NO FEAR

The LORD is my light and my salvation;
>   whom will I fear?
The LORD is the strength of my life;
>   of whom will I be afraid? . . .
Though an army should set up camp and surround me,
>   my heart will not fear:
Though war should rise against me,
>   in this will I be confident. . . .
For in the time of trouble God will hide me in his pavilion:
>   in the secret of his tabernacle will he hide me;
>   he will set me up upon a rock.

PSALM 27:1–5, KJV, ADAPTED

PRAY

Hear, O LORD, when I cry with my voice:
>   *and have mercy on me, and answer me.*
When you said, "Seek my face,"
>   *my heart said to you, "Your face, LORD, will I seek. . . ."*
Wait on the LORD: be of good courage,
>   *and he will strengthen your heart:*
>   *wait, I say, on the LORD.*

PSALM 27:7–8, 14, KJV, ADAPTED

REMEMBER We find courage in the Lord's presence to do whatever we should and must.

SEEING WHAT WE DESIRE

Someone once confided to a friend, "A lot of us assume that by the time we reach age forty, we should have 'gotten it' when it comes to prayer. We should have become settled in a growing life of devotion. Well, if we are honest, most of us admit we haven't." That leaves some people discouraged. But wherever you find yourself in growing closer to God, you don't ever need to let what you have not done keep you from discovering what you can do.

PRAY

O Lord my God,
my creator and my re-creator,
my soul longs for you.
Tell me what you are,
beyond what I have seen,
so that I may see clearly what I desire.[36]
ST. ANSELM, ELEVENTH CENTURY

REMEMBER "God gives many things to us because of his generosity, even without our asking for them. But that he gives certain things to us only when we ask is for our good, that we may gain confidence in coming to God, and that we may recognize him as the Author of all the good things we enjoy" (St. Thomas Aquinas, thirteenth century, adapted).

LIFE'S LITTLE MERCIES

More than we usually see, every day plays host to small miracles and quiet immensities. We see them most clearly through a grateful heart.

PRAY

Lord, I thank you for the little mercies of life:
The pauses that allow me to take a deep breath
  when things grow intense.
The work that absorbs my attention
  and that keeps me from boredom.
The people in this place who know me by name,
  who love me through all my faults.

May I become worthy of the place you have put me,
  the people you have sent into my life,
    the tasks you have entrusted to me.
Amen.

REMEMBER "It is a wise person who does not grieve for things he or she does not have, but rejoices for what he or she has" (Epictetus, first/second century).

WHAT NOT TO FORGET

Bless the LORD, O my soul,
 and all that is within me, bless his holy name.
Bless the LORD, O my soul,
 and forget not all his benefits:
Who forgives all your iniquities;
Who heals all your diseases;
Who redeems your life from destruction;
Who crowns you with lovingkindness and tender mercies;
Who satisfies your mouth with good things;
 so that your youth is renewed like the eagle's.
The LORD executes righteousness and judgment
 for all that are oppressed.
He made known his ways to Moses,
 his acts unto the children of Israel.
The LORD is merciful and gracious,
 slow to anger, and plenteous in mercy.
He will not always chide:
 neither will he keep his anger for ever.
He has not dealt with us according to our sins;
 nor rewarded us according to our iniquities.

PSALM 103:1–10, KJV, ADAPTED

PRAY

*Lord, may I not forget your unfathomable grace and the healing
benefits I enjoy as your child. Amen.*

REMEMBER "For as the heaven is high above the earth, so great
is his mercy toward them that fear him" (Psalm 103:11, KJV,
adapted).

A THANKFUL HEART

"Count your many blessings," counsels an old gospel hymn.
"Count them one by one." Such an arithmetic of gratitude
leads us not to miserly inwardness but to expansive generosity.

PRAY

Lord, I have many things to be thankful for:

A job to do,
A cup of something hot to drink.

A spot to call my own,
Coffee breaks and talking with others.

Coworkers and clients to serve,
People who care for me.

You provide challenges to keep me alert,
But best of all your grace keeps me going.

Amen.

REMEMBER Call to mind often the day's blessings; pass quickly
over the day's troubles.

ABOVE ALL

We pray for many things, and we should. God welcomes our prayers for health, contentment, and good relationships. We need never hesitate to bring to God our daily needs. But if we stop at that, there's so much we will miss.

PRAY

Loving God,
who sees in humankind nothing
that you have not given to us yourself,
make my body healthy and nimble,
my mind acute and clear,
my heart happy and content,
my soul loyal and loving.
And surround me with a crowd of people and angels
who share my devotion to you.

Above all let me live in your presence,
for with you all fear is banished,
and there is only concord and peace.
Let every day combine
the beauty of spring,
the brightness of summer,
the harvest abundance of fall,
and the sleepy quietness of winter.
At the end of my life on earth,
grant that I may come
to see and know you in the fullness of your glory.[37]

ST. THOMAS AQUINAS, THIRTEENTH CENTURY, ADAPTED

REMEMBER As much as possible, throughout today let gentle, short, and passing prayers arise from within you. Remember to ask to experience more of God's presence and glorious goodness.

THE REST OF OUR LIVES

Whether today has you looking behind, wondering what will come, or simply enjoying the present moment, be sure to thank God for his constant mercy and never-failing kindness.

PRAY

Most gracious God, who has been infinitely merciful to us,
not only in the past year,
but through all the years of our life,
be pleased to accept our heartfelt thanks
for your unnumbered blessings to us,
for your graciously forgiving all our shortcomings and sins,
and for your generously developing in us graces and virtues.
And every year you will add to our lives,
add also, we pray,
more strength to our faith,
more fervor to our love,
and a greater depth to our obedience.
Grant that we may,
with humble sincerity and perseverance,
serve you faithfully
the rest of our lives.
Amen.

CHARLES HOW, EIGHTEENTH CENTURY, ADAPTED

REMEMBER "Now to him who by the power at work within us is able to accomplish abundantly far more than all we can ask or imagine, to him be glory in the church and in Christ Jesus to all generations, forever and ever. Amen" (Ephesians 3:20–21).

PRAYER AT WORK

Once, when asked how to pray, a wise spiritual teacher said, "Pick a time, pick a place, and then show up." That advice sounds refreshingly simple. The teacher knew that far more important than the words we use (or stumble over) is a simple decision. Rather than turn prayer into a complicated, out-of-reach regimen, sometimes the important thing is simply to show up, wherever we are, taking advantage of whatever coffee break or lunch hour or commute time we can. We try to still our hearts and minds. And then we turn our thoughts Godward. We let words—our own or those of others—form and guide our devotion.

As you do so, several simple guidelines may help:

Remember that prayer can be uncomplicated and profoundly simple. The point of the Bible's repeated invitations to us to pray ("Ask. . . . Seek. . . . Knock," said Jesus) is that we can come to prayer as we are, even stumbling and stammering. We may not get up from prayer just as we were, but always we begin as we can, not as we cannot. However haltingly, we approach, not so much worried about perfection as determined to move in the right direction.

God, after all, is not a being we must rush after. A relationship with God is not something to manufacture, and intimacy with

God is not something we must win; it is freely offered in Jesus Christ as a gift we receive. Prayer grows naturally out of that grace-filled atmosphere of trust and love. "We approach God through love," said St. Augustine centuries ago, "not navigation."

Remember that slowing down is much of the battle. Work has a way of enveloping us in its relentless demands and priorities. Sometimes we keep our eyes so glued to the project or goal before us that we forget to look up. A simple shift in our gaze, however, can remind us of the wider world around us—faces we like (or need to learn to love), a framed photo of a loved one, perhaps even the gentle light from a window or lamp.

When we are quiet, we can attend to the restlessness that makes us reach out to God. We hear a quiet prompting that draws us into conversation with God. Then we do something to respond. Maybe we pause and look out the window of our office Maybe we close our eyes on the noisy subway. We say to ourselves, "I am going to pray!" And then we begin.

Remember to pray through the distractions. Once we manage to carve out a bit of space for prayer, distractions tempt us to something else—anything else. Poet-preacher John Donne talked about finally sitting down for prayer, inviting "God and his angels" to come. And, he said, "when they are there, I neglect God and his angels for the noise of a fly, for the rattling of a coach, for the whining of a door. . . . Sometimes I find that I had forgot what I was about." Donne concluded, "So certainly there is nothing, nothing in spiritual things, perfect in this world."

Not perfect, but sufficient. When we try to make more room for God, we may fall into the all-or-nothing fallacy: missing opportunities for praying and drawing closer to God because we think only in terms of the big blocks of time and the ideal settings. But we can pray in snatches. Don't assume you have to have long stretches. A Gothic cathedral or a woodland spot are not the only settings for meditating on God. You don't have to have smooth inner (or outer) tranquillity to pray. Your place to pray may be less than pristinely silent. But don't let the fact that you must pray through irritating noises keep you from praying at all.

Remember that prayer can be woven through all of life. "How daily life is!" someone once said. The same can be said about prayer—which means that it belongs in all of life. We can pray our way through noise and traffic and stress and boredom.

A recent article on high achievers noted how many of them compartmentalize their emotions so that they can focus on their work. You may be tempted to do something similar with your spiritual life. But as one woman said, "I would prefer the all-through-the-day prayer approach." Or as nineteenth-century novelist Victor Hugo put it, "There are moments when, whatever be the attitude of the body, the soul is on its knees."

Why not pray now? As you do, don't forget to thank God for making prayer so wonderfully accessible—and ceaselessly promising.

NOTES

1. "Te Deum," in *Eerdmans' Book of Famous Prayers* (Grand Rapids, Mich.: William B. Eerdmans Publishing, 1984), 30.

2. Ray Simpson, comp., *Celtic Blessings* (Chicago: Loyola Press, 1999), 31.

3. Ibid., 108.

4. Ibid., 144.

5. *The Sayings of Light and Love,* in *The Collected Works of St. John of the Cross,* trans. Kieran Kavanaugh and Otilio Rodriquez (Washington, D.C.: ICS Publications, 1991), 97.

6. This quotation was printed on one of the business cards that Mother Teresa handed out.

7. *The Sayings of Light and Love,* 90.

8. Oswald Chambers, *My Utmost for His Highest* (Uhrichsville, Ohio: Barbour, 1963), 50.

9. Paul Wilkes, *Beyond the Walls* (New York: Doubleday, 1999), 9.

10. John Ortberg, "Taking Care of Business," *Leadership,* Fall 1998, 28.

11. Henri Nouwen, *Heart Speaks to Heart* (Notre Dame, Ind.: Ave Maria Press, 1989), 20.

12. *Special Counsels,* in *The Collected Works of St. John of the Cross,* 729.

13. *The Sayings of Light and Love,* 96.

14. The source of this quotation is a letter from Mother Teresa to a monk friend of mine at St. Meinrad's Archabbey.

15. Robert Collyer, quoted in original form in John Heuss, comp., *A Book of Prayers* (New York: Morehouse-Gorham, 1957), 19.

16. *Special Counsels*, 729.

17. *A Prayer Book for Catholic Families* (Chicago: Loyola Press, 1998), 32.

18. Ralph Spaulding Cushman, *A Pocket Prayer Book and Devotional Guide* (Nashville: Upper Room Books, 1941).

19. Dinah Maria Mulock Craik, quoted in Edythe Draper, *Draper's Book of Quotations for the Christian World* (Wheaton, Ill.: Tyndale House Publishers, 1992), 365.

20. St. Ignatius of Loyola, quoted in Gertrud Mueller Nelson and Christopher Witt, eds., *Pocket Prayers* (New York: Doubleday, Image Books, 1995), 30.

21. Although frequently attributed to St. Francis of Assisi, this prayer cannot be traced further back than the nineteenth century. It certainly does, however, reflect the faith and spirit of St. Francis.

22. St. Symeon the New Theologian, quoted in original form in Nelson and Witt, 62.

23. Quoted in Richard Newman, *Go Down, Moses* (New York: Clarkson Potter, 1998), 37.

24. J. R. R. Tolkien, quoted in Draper, 452.

25. Gerard Manley Hopkins, quoted in Draper, 653.

26. Kathy Coffey, *God in the Moment: Making Every Day a Prayer* (Chicago: Loyola Press, 1999), 44, 46.

27. St. Francis of Assisi, quoted in *Eerdmans' Book of Famous Prayers*, 30.

28. Andrew Murray, quoted in Draper.

29. C. S. Lewis, *Letters to Malcolm, Chiefly on Prayer* (San Diego, Calif.: Harcourt Brace Jovanovich, 1964), 17.

30. A. W. Tozer, *The Pursuit of God* (Camp Hill, Penn.: Christian Publications, 1993), 76.

31. Mother Teresa of Calcutta, quoted in Draper, 284.

32. J. Barrie Shepherd, *Aspects of Love: An Exploration of 1 Corinthians 13* (Nashville: Upper Room Books, 1995).

33. E. B. Pusey, quoted in original form in Heuss, 33.

34. St. Thomas Aquinas, quoted in *Eerdmans' Book of Famous Prayers*, 33.

35. St. Gregory of Nazianzus, quoted in original form in Robert Van de Weyer, comp., *The HarperCollins Book of Prayers* (San Francisco: Harper San Francisco, 1993), 174.

36. St. Anselm, quoted in *Prayers across the Centuries*, Vinita Hampton Wright, comp. (Wheaton, Ill.: Harold Shaw Publishers, 1993), 73.

37. St. Thomas Aquinas, quoted in original form in Van de Weyer, 364.